CELEBRATING
JESUS
IN THE
BIBLICAL
FEASTS

EXPANDED EDITION

DESTINY IMAGE BOOKS BY DR. RICHARD BOOKER

Radical Islam's War Against Christianity and the West

Living in His Presence

The Miracle of the Scarlet Thread Revised

Blow the Trumpet in Zion

Discovering the Miracle of the Scarlet Thread in Every Book of the Bible

The Overcomers

The Lamb and the Seven-Sealed Scroll

The Victorious Kingdom

CELEBRATING
JESUS
IN THE
BIBLICAL
FEASTS

Discovering Their Significance to
You as a Christian

Dr. Richard Booker

DESTINY IMAGE® PUBLISHERS, INC.

P.O. Box 310, Shippensburg, PA 17257-0310

"Promoting Inspired Lives."

Previously published as Celebrating Jesus in the Biblical Feasts
Previous ISBN: 978-0-7684-2737-0

This book and all other Destiny Image and Destiny Image Fiction books are available at Christian bookstores and distributors worldwide.

For more information on foreign distributors, call 717-532-3040.

Reach us on the Internet: www.destinyimage.com.

ISBN 13 TP: 978-0-7684-0901-7
ISBN 13 eBook: 978-0-7684-0902-4

For Worldwide Distribution, Printed in the U.S.A.

4 5 6 7 8 / 20 19 18 17 16

CONTENTS

Preface 7

Introduction 13

CHAPTER 1   The Biblical Jewish Calendar 27

CHAPTER 2   Passover 33

CHAPTER 3   Unleavened Bread 63

CHAPTER 4   Firstfruits 79

CHAPTER 5   Pentecost 91

CHAPTER 6   Trumpets 109

CHAPTER 7   Atonement 123

CHAPTER 8   Tabernacles 137

CHAPTER 9   Purim 151

CHAPTER 10   Hanukkah 167

CHAPTER 11   How Christians Celebrate Jesus in the Feasts 179

APPENDIX   Celebrating Jesus in the Passover 199

PREFACE

In the Hebrew Scriptures, God provided a written record of pictures of the Messiah to enable the Jewish people to recognize Him when He appeared. Jesus of Nazareth claimed to be this Messiah and proved it by fulfilling in Himself the very Scriptures and pictures that pointed to the Messiah. Yet, even though many Jews believed that Jesus was the Messiah, the powerful Jewish leadership in Jerusalem, the establishment, rejected Him for themselves and the nation of Israel.

Ironically, the Gentiles embraced Jesus. As the apostle John wrote, "He came to His own, and His own did not receive Him. But as many as received Him, to them He gave the right to become children of God, to those who believe in His name" (John 1:11-12).

These Gentile followers of Jesus experienced a spiritual new birth and became part of a company of people who would be called Christians. These non-Jewish believers did not replace the Jewish people in God's plan of redemption. Instead, they were in-grafted to the Jewish people and became part of the commonwealth of Israel, with Abraham as their spiritual father.

THE GREAT DIVIDE

As the Christian Church (called-out ones) became more "Gentilized," Jews and Christians began to go their separate ways. It wasn't long before the Church (the organized Christian religion) was flooded with unbelievers who embraced the Christian faith but never received Jesus personally as their Lord and Savior. Their hearts did not change. These people brought their hatred of Jews with them into this new Christian faith.

About the same time, some of the early Church fathers (Gentiles not connected to their biblical Hebraic roots) developed a faulty theology that created an anti-Semitic mentality in the Church. This further divided the Christian world from the Jews. These early anti-Jewish declarations laid the foundation for the tragic future of Jewish-Christian relations that would see the Church lose sight of its Jewish roots and persecute the Jews down through the centuries.

GOD IS DOING A NEW THING

But in these last days, God is doing a marvelous thing. He is breaking down the walls of hatred and misunderstanding that have divided the Jews and Christians. God is calling the Jewish people to return to their ancient homeland and to their covenant God. He is preparing them for the coming of the Messiah. At the same time, God is stirring in the hearts of Christians a holy love for the Jewish people and awakening them to the biblical Hebraic-Jewish roots of their Christian faith.

Many Christians are realizing that the origin of our faith is Jerusalem, not Athens, Rome, Geneva, Wittenberg, Aldersgate, Azusa Street, Springfield, Nashville, Tulsa, etc. As a result, Christians around the world are reaching out to the Jewish people in their communities, singing songs from the Hebrew Scriptures, rediscovering their Jewish roots, and celebrating the Sabbath and the Feasts of the Lord as fulfilled in Jesus. It is clearly God's appointed time to reconcile Jews and Christians in preparation for the coming of Messiah.

CELEBRATING JESUS IN THE FEASTS

Because of the prophetic season in which we are living, millions of Christians around the world are realizing that it is proper, good, and pleasing to the Lord to celebrate Jesus in the Feasts. There are a number of benefits Christians are experiencing by doing this. Some of these are:

1. A better understanding of the Bible

2. A rediscovery of the Jewish roots of Christianity

3. A fuller comprehension of God's plan of redemption

4. A renewed passion for Jesus

5. Greater insights into God's prophetic seasons

6. Clearer and more powerful teachings through visual aids

7. A discovery of the biblical Church calendar

8. A love for the Jewish people and understanding of the role of Israel in Bible prophecy and current events

9. Spiritual growth and bonding among family members

What believer would not want these benefits? You can realize them in your own life and congregations by celebrating the Feasts of the Lord as they find their fulfillment in Jesus. This is not something Christians have to do but something we get to do as a way of identifying with Jesus our Jewish Lord. It is a blessing, not a burden. It is an act of love, not legalism.

When Christians celebrate Jesus in the Feasts, they are not "putting themselves under the Law" or trying to be Jews. They are simply expressing their desire to return to the biblical roots of the faith. These desires come from the Spirit of God who birthed them in the heart of the believer. Responding to these desires is wholly a matter of God's grace and not in any way a matter of legalism. Christians who are discovering the biblical Hebraic roots and want to celebrate them should not glory in the pictures but in the person of Jesus.

Paul said, "For whatever things were written before were written for our learning…" (Rom. 15:4). By celebrating Jesus in the Feasts, we can learn more fully what Jesus has done for us and how to walk with Him in our everyday lives.

I am able to say this from my own personal experiences. In 1974, the Lord awakened me spiritually to an awareness that the Hebrew Bible, what we Christians call the Old Testament, was a picture of the person of Jesus of Nazareth. Believe it or not, the Lord showed this to me in the book of Leviticus. God's Word leaped off the pages of the Bible and spiritually exploded in my heart. It was alive with His very life and power inside me. I experienced an immediate, dramatic, lasting change in my life, and I have not been the same from that moment on.

With this revelation burning in my heart, I began to see that the Bible was more than just a collection of unrelated stories. There was a master theme that told one central story through its pages. This central story was that God had taken the initiative to enter into a blood covenant with us through Jesus. God enabled me to see this story in every book of the Bible. The Bible was no longer a dusty old book. It was the living Word of the living God, and it was alive in me. I wrote about this in my book, *The Miracle of the Scarlet Thread*.

When the Lord showed me Jesus in Leviticus, He opened my spiritual eyes to see how Jesus was pictured in the biblical Feasts of the Lord. This incredible revelation has been one of the greatest blessings of my life. My discovery of Jesus in the Feasts has helped me understand the Bible and God's plan of redemption; it has helped me know how to walk with God; it has renewed my passion for Jesus and the many other benefits I just mentioned. The Lord so overwhelmed me with His presence and this insight that I had to share it with others. I left my career at that time and have devoted my life to telling everyone what the Lord had showed me.

I began immediately to teach on the blood covenant and the Feasts of the Lord as pictures of Jesus. It was in the early 1980s that I wrote my book on *Jesus in the Feasts of Israel*. Since that time, the book has had many printings and touched the lives of thousands of readers. Now that more Christians are discovering these wonderful truths for themselves, it seemed like a good thing to release an updated version of this book with the present title. I am grateful to my friends at Destiny Image Publishers for sharing this vision to bring this important work to a new generation of readers.

As you read this book, I pray this powerful blessing into your life from Numbers 6:24-26, "The Lord bless you and keep you; the Lord make His face shine upon you, and be gracious to you; the Lord lift up His countenance upon you, and give you peace."

Introduction

PICTURES OF A PERSON

I'm sure you have heard the expression, "A picture is worth a thousand words." What do we mean by this? Simply that we can more clearly communicate our thoughts and concepts with the use of visual aids than we can with words alone.

For example, if you want to teach a child the alphabet, you don't begin by giving the child a lecture on the theory of language. The child would not be able to understand what you are talking about. Instead, you give the child a block with a letter carved on it. The block is a visual aid to teach the child how to recognize a particular letter of the alphabet.

As the child learns, you give him or her more blocks with other letters until eventually the child has one block for each letter of the alphabet. Soon the child is able to put these blocks together in correct sequence as they correspond to the alphabet and make up single words. The child has now learned the ABCs. The blocks are visual aids used as object lessons to teach the child the alphabet.

In today's world, parents also use computers in place of these physical blocks. But the principle is the same—only now the blocks are electronic. The child learns to point to the picture of the letter on the computer. A computer tutorial communicates to the child if he or she gave the right answer.

GOD'S VISUAL AIDS

In the Bible, God often used visual aids as object lessons to teach us spiritual truths that He wanted us to understand. God used these visual aids as pictures in much the same manner that we would use the blocks to teach our children the alphabet. God has done this because in our fallen, sinful condition, it is difficult for us to understand spiritual truths. We perceive things through our physical senses much more clearly than we do through our spiritual senses.

In view of this, when God began to teach His covenant people, the Jews, He did so through the use of visual aids or pictures that the Jews could comprehend with their physical senses. God gave these pictures in the Hebrew Bible in the form of the various religious laws and rituals that the Jews were to observe. (I will be using the term *Hebrew Bible* rather than *Old Testament* throughout this book.) As the Jews practiced these laws and rituals, they would learn spiritual truths concerning their relationship with God through their physical senses.

For 1,500 years, the Jewish people learned about the one true God through their visual aids. Their religious laws and rituals taught them how to know God and walk with Him on a daily basis. They also pointed them to the Messiah. But just as the child's blocks are not the real alphabet, neither were these physical pictures complete in themselves. They were important, but they were only pictures.

THE ULTIMATE VISUAL AID

After centuries of looking at the pictures, the time came when the Jews were to enter into the spiritual reality of these visual aids. The transition from the physical to the spiritual was provided for them through Jesus of Nazareth, the Jewish Messiah and Savior of the world. While the Hebrew Scriptures provided the pictures, the New Testament provided the person. In other words, the pictures in the Hebrew Bible pointed to the person in the New Testament.

This picture-to-person connection is what Jesus was referring to in Matthew 5:17-18 when He said, "Do not think that I came to destroy the Law or the Prophets. I did not come to destroy but to fulfill. For assuredly, I say to you, till heaven and earth pass away, one jot or one tittle will by no means pass from the law till all is fulfilled."

Because the common western understanding of *fulfill* means "done away with," Christians have believed that Jesus meant the pictures pointing to Him were no longer needed. This is not what Jesus meant. We have to understand His words in the context of His Jewish culture and customs.

To Jewish Bible teachers and rabbis in the time of Jesus, the word that is translated into English as *fulfilled* meant the true or correct interpretation of Scripture, while the word *destroy* meant to give a false or incorrect interpretation. These words were used in a technical sense by the Jewish religious leaders when arguing over the correct meaning of Scriptures.[1]

In New Testament times, Jewish Bible teachers and rabbis, like Christian Bible teachers and ministers today, often studied the Scriptures together. As they discussed a certain Scripture, each would give his opinion of what he thought the Scripture meant.

One might say, "I believe this Scripture means such-and-such." Inevitably someone in the study group would disagree. He would then say, "No, that is not correct. You are not correctly interpreting this Scripture. You are doing away with or destroying the Scripture." Then another in the group would say, "No, he is fulfilling the Scripture. He is giving the true meaning of the Scripture."

When Jesus used the words *fulfill* and *destroy*, He was speaking in terms that were used by the religious leaders of His time. They understood exactly what He meant. He was telling them that He did not come to do away with or destroy (lead them astray by false teachings) the Hebrew Scriptures. Instead, He fulfilled them as the person to whom the pictures were pointing. He was the human embodiment of their true meaning and spiritual reality.

A *jot* is the Hebrew character called the *yod* and is the smallest of the Hebrew alphabet. The *tittle* is a tiny mark used to distinguish certain Hebrew letters. By making such a reference, Jesus is showing how He honored and fulfilled even the least of all that was written of Him in the Hebrew Scriptures.

Unfortunately, we Christians living in the western world are the ones who have unwittingly destroyed (incorrectly understood) God's pictures. We have done this by interpreting the words of Jesus through western eyes rather than understanding Jesus as a Jewish Bible teacher of His times. We have done this with good intentions, but the result has been a great loss of the pictures that point us to the person. But now we are living in the most exciting time of spiritual history, when God is awakening Christians around the world to the importance of understanding the Scriptures in their cultural context and the spiritual pictures of our Lord.

I want to share a remarkable story that relates to the importance of understanding Jesus in His Jewish context. This is true story about a young Jewish boy named Issur Danielovitch.

Issur was the son of a Russian Jew. He grew up in a harsh childhood of poverty in New York where he was often tormented by the neighborhood "Christian" bully. As an adult, Issur was a secular Jew who found success, fame, and wealth beyond his wildest dreams. God was definitely not a part of his life.

On February 13, 1991, Issur was in a helicopter crash in which two people died, yet he miraculously survived. As he contemplated why he survived, Issur began his personal search for the meaning of life, his own relationship with God, and his identity as a Jew.

As part of his search, Issur read the New Testament, which is a forbidden book to Jews. He explains, "So how did my road back begin? Here's a shocker—with Jesus. Then I found out that Jesus was a Jew! Wow! Then I found out that Jesus was not only a Jew, but a rabbi who gave sermons on the Torah. Do Christians know that? Some things that Jesus said made more sense in the context of Judaism than Christianity. Of all the things I read of him, the one that influenced me most was this speech of Jesus recorded by the gospel writer of Matthew."[2] Issur then quotes Matthew 5:17-19.

Issur Danielovitch's real name is Kirk Douglas. Yes, Kirk Douglas, one of the most famous movie stars in the history of Hollywood, found his Jewish identity when he realized that Jesus is a Jewish rabbi teaching the Torah. While Kirk did not acknowledge Jesus as Messiah, he did return to his Jewish roots and found a new spirituality and purpose for his life.

When we as Christians discover Jesus in His Jewish context, we too will find a new spirituality through the Torah pictures that point to Him as Messiah. The pictures are powerful visuals of the person and redemptive work of Jesus.

Jesus' name in Hebrew is *Yeshua. Christ* comes from the Greek word *christos* and means the same as the Hebrew word for Messiah, which is *mashiach*.[3] To help us keep Jesus in His Jewish context and properly connected to His pictures, I have put *Yeshua the Messiah* in brackets when our English Bible uses the name *Jesus Christ*.

Humans need pictures to help us understand the world around us. The visual aids God gave to the Jewish people were spiritual pictures pointing them to Messiah Jesus. Jesus was God's ultimate visual aid. He was the perfect revelation of the spiritual meaning of the pictures. Jesus said to one of His followers, "...He who has seen Me has seen the Father..." (John 14:9).

Now that the person has come, there is no need to seek God through religious rituals. In fact, God never gave the pictures as objects of affection. Their purpose was to point the people to the person. That is what the apostle Paul meant when he said, "For Christ [Messiah] is the end [goal] of the law for righteousness to everyone who believes" (Rom. 10:4). The words translated into English as "the end" do not mean no longer needed or useful. They mean "the goal."[4] Jesus is the goal of the pictures that were pointing to Him.

This does not mean, however, that the pictures are no longer valuable to us. They still are important in helping us to understand how to know God and walk with Him through a personal relationship with Jesus. Simply put, we can know the person better by studying the pictures.

Focusing on the pictures rather than the person is religion. Focusing on the person is relationship. We have a relationship with the person, but the pictures help us better know the person.

I have been married for over 40 years to the same wonderful woman. I have pictures of her throughout the house. When she walks into the room, I do not turn down her picture as if I no longer needed it because she is in the room. I look at her picture when she is not with me because I love her and want to see her face.

In a similar way, just because Jesus has come into the room of our heart does not mean we no longer need the spiritual pictures pointing us to Him. We need them, not for salvation, but as visual reminders of who He is and what He has done for us. They help keep us focused on the person and provide us with powerful pictures of our Lord, whom we do not yet see face to face.

Christians can certainly relate to the importance of spiritual pictures. For example, water baptism and communion are two powerful visual aids that point us to the person and work of Jesus. We outwardly express our relationship to Jesus through these rituals. The ritual pictures don't save us, but they are significant in keeping us focused on our relationship to our Lord while reminding us what He has done for us. We would never think about doing away with the pictures or that we no longer need them.

THE FEASTS OF THE LORD

Some of the clearest visual aids that God gives in the Bible are the biblical holy days. For centuries, Christians were told that these spiritual pictures were "Jewish Feasts" that Jesus fulfilled (did away with). We have just learned that this is a misinterpretation of what Jesus meant. As we will see, the Bible refers to these religious holy days as the "Feasts of the Lord," not the "Feasts of the Jews."

Most Christians are truly surprised and amazed when they learn that God made reference to His special holy days in the very first chapter of the Book of Genesis. It was the fourth day of creation where we read, "Then God said, 'Let there be lights in the firmament of the heavens to divide the day from the night; and let them be for signs and seasons, and for days and years'" (Gen. 1:14).

The Hebrew word translated into English as "seasons" is *moed*. This word means a fixed, appointed time or season or place when God would meet with His people. It specifically refers to God's appointed biblical holy days. They are His holy festivals or feast days when the people would have a holy encounter with the Living God.[5]

Moed is the same word used to refer to the Feasts of the Lord in the Book of Leviticus. God established these special celebrations when He brought the Hebrews out of Egypt. God spoke to Moses, saying, "Speak to the children of Israel and say to them, 'The feasts of the Lord, which you shall proclaim to be holy convocations, these are My feasts.... These are the feasts of the Lord, holy convocations which you shall proclaim at their appointed times'" (Lev. 23:2,4)

When we hear the word *feast* we think of an elaborate meal or banquet. We tend to associate the word with food. After teaching and writing on this subject for over thirty years, I am still flabbergasted when Christians tell me they thought these biblical holy days had something to do with Jews and eating.

Notice that God said these are His feasts. God's covenant name in the Bible is YHWH (Yahweh). These are the Feasts of YHWH. They were special holy convocations or assemblies established by God when the Jewish people would come together to meet with God in a special way. We might think of them as religious gatherings.

The Hebrew word for a "holy convocation" or "sacred assembly" is *mikrah*. This word means a "dress rehearsal."[6] The Jews would act out through the festivals a dress rehearsal for the purpose of revealing the Messiah and learning the overall redemptive and prophetic plan of God. In other words, for 1,500 years, the Jews performed the drama of redemption as a picture pointing them to the person of Messiah Jesus.

God appointed three feast seasons with seven individual feasts and scheduled them on the Hebrew calendar in such a way that the Jews would have to travel to Jerusalem three times a year to keep them. (See Exodus 23:14-17 and Deuteronomy 16:16.)

These three feast seasons were known as Passover (Pesach), Pentecost (Shavuot), and Tabernacles (Succot). They portrayed and represented three major encounters with God in the lives of His covenant people. These encounters with God were for the purpose of providing His divine peace, power, and rest in their lives. Taken together, they represent seven steps in the believer's walk with God.

The Feast of Passover was the first of these feast seasons. Its purpose was to teach the Hebrews how to find God's peace. Passover included the Feasts of Passover, Unleavened Bread, and Firstfruits.

The next feast season was Pentecost. This was a single feast, and it taught the Hebrews how to receive God's power.

The third feast season was called Tabernacles. The purpose of the Feast of Tabernacles was to teach the people how to enter God's rest. It included the Feasts of Trumpets, Atonement, and Tabernacles.

The Feasts of the Lord were very important visual aids for the Jewish people. Each of the seven feasts pointed them to their Messiah, and each uniquely portrayed a particular aspect of His life and ministry. Taken as a whole, they form a complete picture of the person and work of the Messiah and the steps one must take to walk in the peace, power, and rest of God. Christians have a revelation in their hearts from God's Spirit that Jesus is the Messiah.

Jesus not only celebrated these festivals Himself, but every major redemptive event in His life also happened on a feast day. Wow! Now since Jesus celebrated these festivals and was the spiritual reality of all of them, doesn't it seem important to learn how these pictures pointed to Him and what they can mean for us? And since these are the Feasts of the Lord, wouldn't it be good for all of God's covenant people to celebrate Jesus through these exciting pictures? And since we all need God's peace, power, and rest, wouldn't it be beneficial for believers to understand how the pictures can help us internalize the redemptive work of Jesus in our lives?

WHY I WROTE THIS BOOK

Our world today is no different from the world of the Bible in that we all are still seeking peace. Nations are frantically seeking peace to avoid a nuclear holocaust. Israel is trying in vain to live in peace with her neighbors. Individuals are seeking peace within themselves, peace with God, and peace in their relationships. We will never have peace until we submit our lives to the God of Abraham, Isaac, and Jacob. The Feast of Passover teaches us how to have peace with God through a personal relationship with Jesus as our Passover Lamb.

Everyone who has this personal relationship with Jesus has peace with God. But unfortunately, not all followers of Jesus have the peace of God. Many believers are overcome by fear, worry, and anxiety. Through the Feast of Passover, season of Unleavened Bread, and Firstfruits, we not only learn how to have peace with God but also the peace of God.

We not only need God's peace; we also need God's power. The Bible and human experience tell us that mankind is hopelessly enslaved to self-destructive habits. No matter how many New Year's resolutions we make, it seems we just are not able to keep them. Sin has a hold on us, and only God can set us free!

Psalm 62:11 says that "power belongs to God." God has made His power available to us through Messiah Jesus. Yet, not every believer is walking in the power of Jesus. Many are still overcome by sin, satan, and the fear of death. The Feast of Pentecost teaches us how to receive the power of God and appropriate it in our everyday lives.

We not only need God's peace and power; we also need God's rest. Our brief journey on this earth is but a fleeting moment in which we constantly war against the attacks of the world on our soul. Things don't always turn out the way we hope they will. Life is full of disappointments, heartaches, burdens, and trials. Even believers sometimes grow weary in serving God and coping with the trials and struggles of life. Many are just plain worn out. The Feast of Tabernacles teaches us how to find God's rest for our souls in this life.

The quest for peace, power, and rest for our souls is surely the most elusive and difficult challenge we all face as imperfect humans living in an imperfect world. Yet, God has provided the means for us to live victoriously through the good and bad of life's experiences. I wrote this book to help you learn how to encounter the

Living God in such a way that you will walk in His divine peace, power, and rest.

A LOOK AT WHAT'S AHEAD

You'll begin in Chapter 1 with an overview of the biblical Jewish calendar. You might well ask, "What in the world does the Jewish calendar have to do with my having God's peace, God's power, and God's rest for my soul?" The answer is simply that God established His appointed feasts, His moed, on the Jewish calendar to be celebrated at a certain time and in a certain sequence.

The reason God did this was that Jesus the Messiah was to fulfill them (embody their true spiritual purpose and meaning) in His own life and ministry on the exact dates that the Jews had been celebrating them for 1,500 years. Jesus fulfilled the first two feast seasons (Passover and Pentecost) at His first coming. He will fulfill the third feast season (Tabernacles) at His second coming. This means there is a tremendous amount of prophetic significance in the Jewish calendar. The time and sequence of these feasts reveal the overall prophetic plan of God.

As a believer, it is most important to understand the Jewish calendar for the purpose of learning how to apply the spiritual truths pictured in the feasts to your personal life. As stated, they are pictures of Jesus that teach us how to know Him and walk with Him.

Then in the chapters that follow, we'll study each feast in detail. We'll look back into the Hebrew Scriptures and see exactly what God told the Jews to do and how they celebrated each feast. Then we will look into the New Testament and discover how Jesus fulfilled the feast. After making this connection, you'll learn how to apply what Jesus accomplished for your own life. Finally, you will see how God has been restoring the spiritual realities of these feasts through the history of the Church.

In addition, there is a personal study review at the end of each chapter to assist you in highlighting and reinforcing what you learned. You can complete the personal study review on an individual or group basis.

Psalm 89:15 says, "Blessed are the people who know the joyful sound! They walk, O Lord, in the light of Your countenance." The phrase "joyful sound" refers to the sounding of the shofar to call people to understand and enter into the spiritual realities of the feasts.

Father in Heaven, bless the person reading this book with a divine impartation to hear the joyful sound of Your peace, Your power, and Your rest. Amen!

PERSONAL STUDY REVIEW

1. Why did God use visual aids in the Hebrew Bible?

2. What did Jesus say about His relationship to the Hebrew Bible and the Torah?

3. Explain the meaning of the following Hebrew words:

   A. Moed

   B. Mikrah

4. What are the Feasts of the Lord?

5. Name the three feasts seasons.

6. Name the seven feasts in their order of observance.

ENDNOTES

1. "God's Visual Aids, Point Us to the Messiah," All The Kings Men, September 21, 2014, http://allthekingsmensministries .com/tag/sefartic/.

2. Kirk Douglas, *Climbing the Mountain* (New York, NY: Simon & Schuster, 2000), 118–124.

3. "Strong's #5547, Christós," StudyLight.org, accessed July 01, 2015, http://www.studylight.org/lexicons/greek/gwview. cgi?n=5547; Ibid., "Strong's #4899, mâshîyach," http://www .studylight.org/lexicons/hebrew/hwview.cgi?n=04899.

4. "Telos (philosophy)," Wikipedia, accessed July 01, 2015, https:// en.wikipedia.org/wiki/Telos_%28philosophy%29.

5. "Strong's #4150, mo'êd," StudyLight.org, accessed July 01, 2015, http://www.studylight.org/lexicons/hebrew/hwview. cgi?n=04150.

6. Peter Steffens, "The Origin of Our Weekly Church Service," Peter and Vanessa Steffens, Holy convocation: Mikrah Kodesh, accessed July 01, 2015, http://www.petersteffens.com/articles/ teachings/the-origin-of-our-weekly-church-service.html.

CHAPTER 1

THE BIBLICAL
JEWISH CALENDAR

The standardized calendar used by the world today is known as the Gregorian calendar. This calendar gets it name from Pope Gregory XIII who established it in 1582. This is a sun or "solar" calendar due to the fact that it operates on the principle of the earth revolving around the sun. The different seasons we enjoy are caused by the changing position of the earth as it makes its course around the sun.

As we know, the days on this calendar begin at midnight and last for 24 hours. It takes approximately 365¼ days for the earth to make a complete circle around the sun. This is how we determine the length of the year on the Gregorian calendar. However, some adjustment must be made for the extra quarter of a day. This is why we add an extra day every four years make a leap year of 366 days.

The biblical, or Jewish, calendar is a moon or "lunar" calendar based on the movement of the moon around the earth. The days on this calendar begin at sundown (approximately 6:00 P.M.) and also last for 24 hours. It takes approximately 29½ days for the moon to make a complete circle around the earth. Twelve of these lunar months add up to about 354 days in a lunar year.

The difference in the calendars means that the solar year is 11¼ days longer than the lunar year. This difference requires the Jewish people to make adjustments to their calendar, or else, after a few years, they would be celebrating their feast days in the wrong season of the year.

As we have noted in the previous chapter, God set fixed times and seasons when the Jews were to keep their feasts (see Leviticus 23:4). For example, He told them to celebrate the Feast of Passover during the spring time of the year (see Exodus 12:1-11 and Ezekiel 45:21). If the Jews did not periodically adjust their calendar, they would miss spring by an additional 11¼ days each year. After five years they would be celebrating Passover 56¼ days late and completely out of season.

To compensate for this yearly difference of 11¼ days, the Jewish calendar also has a leap year. Instead of adding an extra day every fourth year as on the Gregorian calendar, they add an extra month at the end of every third year. This inter-calendar month is 29½ days long and makes up most of the difference between the two calendars. This adjustment enables the Jewish people to keep their feast days in the seasons called for by God.

Let's now take a look at the Jewish calendar for the purpose of getting a basic understanding of how it is organized. A copy of the calendar is provided at the end of this chapter. You will need to refer to it for this discussion.

THE SACRED CALENDAR

Notice that the Jews had two concurrent calendar years. One was a sacred calendar which God established when He brought them out of Egypt. We learn in Exodus 12:2 that God told them their deliverance from Egypt was to be the beginning of the sacred calendar and that Nisan would be the first month of the year on this calendar. This month was originally called Abib but later was changed to Nisan during the Babylonian captivity. You can see from the calendar that Nisan corresponds to the months of March and April on the Gregorian calendar. Each month on the lunar calendar may come in one or two Gregorian months because of the 11¼ days difference between the two calendars.

THE CIVIL CALENDAR

The other calendar year was the civil calendar based on the Jews' agricultural season. The civil calendar begins with the month of Tishri, which corresponds to the months of September and October. This is the beginning of the agricultural season.

Notice that the civil calendar and agricultural season began with the early rains that softened the ground for plowing that was done in October and November. This was followed by the sowing of the wheat and barley seed in November and December. The winter rains came in December and January to keep the ground moist. This was followed by the blossoming of the almond trees in January and February, and the citrus harvest in February and March.

The spring or latter rains fell in March and April, concurrent with the beginning of the barley harvest. The dry season was from April-May to September-October. The barley harvest lasted through the spring months and was followed by the wheat harvest in May-June. The grape harvest came next during the months of June-July. July and August was the time of the olive harvest. The season ended with the harvest of dates and figs in August-September.

THE FEASTS SEASONS

Notice that Passover was the first feast celebrated and represented the first of the three major encounters with God in the lives of His covenant people. For this reason, the sacred calendar begins with Passover in the month of Nisan (March-April). This was celebrated during the barley harvest. These feast seasons were visual aids showing the Jewish people how to know God and walk with Him. And as we have said, they were pictures of the Messiah. The spiritual truths symbolized by the feasts are available to all who encounter God through a personal relationship with Jesus the Messiah.

As Christian believers, the very first encounter we have with God through Jesus brings us forgiveness of sin and reconciliation with our Creator-God. The result is that we have peace with God as well as the peace of God. For this reason, the Feast of Passover is the first feast celebrated on the sacred biblical Jewish calendar.

The Feast of Pentecost was celebrated next because it represented the second major encounter with God, which is His power. We all need the power of God working in our lives. Once we have peace with God through our personal relationship with Jesus, we can experience His power. For this reason, the Feast of Pentecost was the second feast celebrated on the sacred calendar. It came at the time of the wheat harvest in the month of *Sivan* (May-June).

The Feast of Tabernacles was celebrated last, at the end of the agricultural season and the beginning of the new one. This was during the lunar month of *Tishri* (September-October). God placed it in this position on the sacred calendar because it represented His third and last encounter in the lives of His people. This final encounter with God represents that place in our walk with God where we find His divine rest for our soul. God's peace comes first, then God's power, then God's rest.

Jewish Calendar				
Sacred	Civil	Name of Months	Farm Season	Feast
1	7	Nisan–Mar-Apr	Barley Harvest	Passover
2	8	Iyyar–Apr-May	Barley Harvest	
3	9	Sivan–May-Jun	Wheat Harvest	Pentecost
4	10	Tammuz–Jun-Jul	Grape Harvest	
5	11	Ab–Jul-Aug	Olive Harvest	
6	12	Elul–Aug-Sept	Dates-Figs Harvest	
7	1	Tishri–Sept-Oct	Early Rains	Tabernacles
8	2	Heshvan–Oct-Nov	Plowing	
9	3	Kieslev–Nov-Dec	Wheat-Barley Sowing	
10	4	Tebeth–Dec-Jan	Winter Rains	
11	5	Shebat–Jan-Feb	Almond Bloom	
12	6	Adar–Feb-Mar	Citrus Harvest (Latter Rains)	
13	—	Adar Sheni	Intercalary Month	

A study of the sacred calendar is certainly not important in itself. Our knowledge of it is for the purpose of understanding God's plan of redemption and salvation for mankind through the person and work of Jesus. As we study the feasts in the following chapters, we will see very clearly that God does have a plan for redeeming all who will come to Him through Messiah Jesus.

Through our study of the feasts, we will learn that God's plan for working out His redemption has a definite beginning, a definite process, and a definite conclusion. This relates not only to the person and work of Jesus our Lord and Savior, but also to our lives as believers. They are pictures that teach us how to walk with God and how God works through history to redeem mankind as revealed in His prophetic seasons.

PERSONAL STUDY REVIEW

1. Explain the difference between the biblical Jewish calendar and the standardized calendar used by the world.

2. Name the two concurrent calendar years used by the Jews.

3. List the three feast seasons in the order in which they were celebrated.

CHAPTER 2

PASSOVER

There are two charts at the end of this chapter. The first chart is titled The Feasts of the Lord. This chart highlights the main aspects of each feast and will help you understand more clearly the teachings in this book. You will need to refer to this chart as we discuss the individual feasts in detail in each chapter. The second chart is titled When Was Jesus Crucified and Resurrected? You will need to refer to it in the chapters on Passover, Unleavened Bread, and Firstfruits. I will explain this chart later in this chapter.

Turn to the page showing *The Feasts of the Lord* chart. Notice there are six columns, each with their respective headings. The first two columns tell you when the feasts are celebrated. The farming season and respective Hebrew months are shown along with the specific dates on which the feasts were celebrated.

The next four columns show the four aspects that we will be discussing for each feast. They are the main focus of this book. In the first column, we will discuss the historical aspect of the feast. We will do this by examining the instructions God gave the Jews for celebrating the feast. Then we will look into the New Testament and see how Jesus fulfilled (embodied the spiritual reality) what the feast symbolized.

Next, we will learn how to apply this work of Jesus to our own life. This is the personal application and represents the seven steps to Christian maturity and God's rest. Finally, we will consider the seasonal aspect of the feast, which will show us its prophetic significance and how God has been restoring the spiritual truths of the feast to the Church. Let's begin now with the Feast of Passover (*Pesach* in Hebrew).

HISTORICAL BACKGROUND

Passover was the first of the three feast seasons. All Jewish males were required to journey to Jerusalem for a special encounter with and visitation from God. Notice from the chart that it was celebrated during the barley harvest in the month of Nisan. The instructions for celebrating the feasts are found throughout the Hebrew Scriptures. Leviticus 23 gives a good summary of them all. Numbers 28-29 and Deuteronomy 16 also provide a good summary.

Let's now consider the historical aspects of Passover. We read in Leviticus, "These are the feasts of the Lord, holy convocations which you shall proclaim at their appointed times. On the fourteenth day of the first month at twilight [evening] is the Lord's Passover" (Lev. 23:4-5).

The Passover was to be a memorial to the Hebrews' deliverance from Egypt. This deliverance happened during the month of *Nisan* and represented God's first encounter with His covenant people. (See Exodus 12:1-14; 43-48.)

You recall that God chose Moses as His instrument to lead the Hebrews out of bondage. Working through Moses, God sent ten terrible plagues against Egypt. This was God's way of convincing Pharaoh to let the Hebrews go. But each time God sent a new plague, Pharaoh's heart hardened (see Exod. 3-10).

God gave Pharaoh every chance to let the Hebrews go, but Pharaoh would not yield. God then declared a tenth and final plague, which was the death of the firstborn of every family (see Exod. 11). But along with this decree of death, God gave specific instructions on how to be saved from this death.

The complete record of this culminating event, which resulted in the Hebrews' deliverance from Egypt, is recorded in the Book of Exodus. If you have a Bible, it would be good to take a moment and read that account before continuing with this chapter. The specific Scriptures to read are Exodus 12:1-14; 43-48.

Let's summarize what God said for the purpose of spotlighting certain key points of His instructions. Every man was to select for his household a lamb without spot or blemish. He was to select this lamb on the tenth day of the month. Then he was to observe this lamb for five days to make sure there was nothing wrong with him. There could be no fault (spot or blemish) found in this lamb.

On the fifth day, he was to bring the lamb to his doorstep and kill him. As he killed the lamb, he would catch the blood in the basin at the foot of the doorstep. Then he would sprinkle the blood on both sides of the doorpost and above the doorpost. Thus, the entire entrance into the house was covered by the blood of the lamb.

This was done on the evening of the 14th day (twilight). We have already mentioned that the Hebrew day begins in the evening at approximately six o'clock. The Hebrews killed the lambs at three o'clock in the afternoon on the 14th in order to eat the meal by six.

When three o'clock arrived, they slaughtered the lamb and applied the blood to their doorpost. The family then entered their house through the blood-stained door where they were protected from the plague of death that was to move through the land.

According to the instructions, the entire lamb was to be roasted and consumed. Nothing could be left over for the next day. In preparing the meal, not one bone of the lamb was to be broken. This instruction required that the lamb be roasted on a spit shaped like a crossbar so that its body could be spread open.

Although the family went inside the house and couldn't see the blood covering, they had faith that God would save them because of it. They were saved by grace through faith in the blood of the lamb, which they could not see.

As they ate the meal, God allowed the angel of death to pass through the land. As he passed from door to door, he sought to enter every household. If the entrance was covered by blood, the angel of death could not enter but had to pass over that house. If the entrance was not covered by blood, judgment would come upon that household as the firstborn would die.

This was the Lord's Passover. We see that He used the blood of the lamb to save His people from death. The blood of the lamb was their covering and protection.

I mentioned in the previous chapter that the Hebrew word for Passover is *Pesach*. This word means to come under the protection of a deity by crossing over, jumping over, stepping over, or leaping over something, in this case, the threshold.[1] Humankind's earliest primitive altar to the one true God, as well as false gods, was the threshold or entrance into the home. The threshold altar was the place where people made their sacrifice to their gods. The purpose was to request protection from the family deity as well as inviting the deity into their house.

When people dedicated their house to their god, they did so by making a sacrifice at the threshold. So it was the common practice to kill an animal at the threshold of the house as the way of welcoming the family deity. They would then cross over the threshold and enter the house.

Since the people were making a sacred blood covenant with their god, they were careful to cross over, step over, leap over, or jump over the blood. To trample under foot the blood was to show contempt and rejection of the covenant. They would then invite the deity into their house to be their protector and provider. In their way of thinking, because they dedicated the house to their god at the blood-stained threshold, their god stood in the doorway protecting them from harm.

The common understanding of Passover that has come down to us over the centuries is that God somehow passed by the dwellings where the blood was applied. But the biblical understanding is much more powerful. When the people applied the blood to the threshold and doorway, they were inviting God to pass over or cross over the threshold into their house as their protector from the angel of death. God, in a sense, stood in the doorway protecting the people from death. He entered into a threshold-blood covenant with the people as He crossed over the blood-stained threshold while His executioner entered the houses of those who did not have the blood. This Passover was actually a Crossing Over or Threshold Covenant.

God further instructed that no uncircumcised person could partake of the Passover meal or celebrate the feast (see Exod. 12:48). The significance of this was that circumcision was the outward evidence that the person was in covenant with God. It showed that the individual had accepted the God of the Hebrews as the one true God and had entered into a blood covenant with Him.

Thus if a Gentile came to accept the God of the Hebrews for himself, he had to be circumcised. He would then be considered as one born in the land. This means that he would be an heir to the promises God made to Abraham and could inherit the blessings that were part of God's covenant with the Jewish people.

Later, when the temple was built, instead of killing the lambs at the doorpost, the people would bring their lambs to Jerusalem and kill them at the temple. They looked forward to this every year. The entire Jewish nation converged on Jerusalem from all corners of the ancient world.

The pilgrims came in caravans, numbering hundreds of participants, sometimes thousands. The caravan leaders would awaken the travelers each morning with the following loud wake-up call, "Arise, and let us go up to Zion, to the Lord our God" (Jer. 31:6).

The festival pilgrims faced many dangers as they made their journey to Jerusalem. Robbers waited to ambush them, for they knew of the money the pilgrims carried for the temple in Jerusalem. Accordingly, the Jews traveled in large, armed groups. Some traveled for many weeks, while the residents of Jerusalem busied themselves with preparations for the arrival of the great throngs of pilgrims.

The preparations in Jerusalem began early. It was especially important to repair the roads and ritual baths, and to mark gravesites clearly to protect the pilgrims from exposure to ritual impurity. Everything was done to make sure the pilgrims arrived on time. It would be terrible to come this far just to "miss the big event."

With so many people coming to Jerusalem, it was necessary to set up ovens throughout the city. After the sacrifice was offered, it was taken by each family and group, roasted in a special manner, and then eaten in the evening. It took months to prepare these ovens.

The Passover celebration was a time of great joy, praise, and worship to God. As they sacrificed at the temple, the Levites would lead the people in singing the Psalms of David, specifically Psalms 113-118. They began by all singing the first line of each Psalm. Then the Levites would sing the second line of each Psalm, and the people would respond by saying, "Hallelujah" or "Praise the Lord."

The singing was accompanied with musical instruments of trumpets, harps, flutes, tambourines, cymbals, and other instruments. It reached its peak as the worshipers lifted their voices to God and sang, "This is the day the Lord has made; we will rejoice and be glad in it" (Ps. 118:24).[2]

As time passed, it became more difficult for the people in the outlying regions to bring their sacrifice to Jerusalem. To solve this problem, the Levites began raising lambs for the Passover sacrifice right in Jerusalem and selling them at the temple. In this way, the pilgrims could buy a lamb already set aside for sacrifice. It would be a lamb without spot or blemish, and it was born to die as a Passover lamb. The Jewish historian Josephus reported there were more than 250,000 of these Passover lambs killed in Jerusalem in the first century.[3]

HOW JESUS FULFILLED THE FEAST

For 1,500 years the Jewish people had been celebrating the Feast of Passover by killing a lamb and offering it as a sacrifice to God. They knew about lambs. But the blood of an animal could only cover their sins; it could not take them away. In view of this, God sent prophets to explain to the people that, one day in the future, a human lamb would come who would deal with the problem of sin and death once and for all.

The prophet Isaiah spoke of the suffering this human lamb would experience. He wrote a very clear, graphic description, which is recorded in Isaiah chapter 53. It would be helpful to read that entire chapter as part of this study.

As the time came for this human lamb to be sacrificed, God crossed over time and space and became one of us in the person of Jesus of Nazareth. God sent one last prophet to help the people recognize Him. This prophet was John the Baptist, the forerunner of Jesus. John introduced Jesus with these words: "Behold the Lamb of God!" (John 1:36).

John identified Jesus as the human lamb Isaiah spoke of who would give His life for the sins of the world. Jesus was born for this purpose (see Acts 2:22-23). Because of their religious sacrifices, the

Jewish people immediately understood the significance of John's statements concerning Jesus.

You will notice in the *Feasts of the Lord* chart that Jesus fulfilled the Feast of Passover in His crucifixion. Since this was the reason for His birth, Jesus' entire life was predestined so that He would fulfill this purpose exactly as God had instructed the Jews to practice it for 1,500 years. As said in the introductory chapter, the picture pointed to the person.

In view of this, as the time approached for Jesus to die, He deliberately arranged His itinerary and personal activities around the events associated with the selection, testing, and death of the Passover Lamb. In this way, the Jewish people would be able to understand who He was and what He was doing. They had acted out the drama of redemption through the Passover picture. Jesus was set aside to be sacrificed, examined, and crucified on the exact month, day, and hour that the Jews had been handling the lambs for 1,500 years in keeping the Feast of Passover.

Let's now see this for ourselves in the New Testament. When God established the Passover feast in Egypt, He instructed the Jews to set aside their lambs on the tenth day of the month of *Nisan*. In the New Testament we learn that it was the tenth day of the month of *Nisan* when Jesus entered Jerusalem to be set aside as the human lamb.

In John 12:1 we read that Jesus came to the town of Bethany six days before the Passover. John writes, "Then, six days before the Passover, Jesus came to Bethany..." (John 12:1). Since Passover was celebrated on the 14th, this would mean that Jesus came to Bethany on the ninth.

John then gives us further information to show us that Jesus entered Jerusalem on the tenth. He says,

> *"The next day a great multitude that had come to the feast, when they heard that Jesus was coming to*

Jerusalem, took branches of palm trees and went out to meet Him, and cried out: 'Hosanna! Blessed is He who comes in the name of the Lord!'" (John 12:12-13).

John informs us that it was the next day when Jesus rode into Jerusalem and was greeted by the cheering crowds. Since Jesus was in Bethany on the ninth, the next day was the tenth.

Jesus entered Jerusalem to be set aside as the human Lamb of God on the exact date that God told the Jews to set aside their lambs back in Egypt. Jesus was fulfilling in Himself the ultimate reality of the Feast of Passover.

As we have mentioned, the purpose of setting the lamb aside was to observe it to make sure it was without spot or blemish. This lamb was to be offered to God. Since God is perfect, you certainly wouldn't offer Him a lamb that was blemished. So the Jews observed and tested the lamb for five days to make sure that it was faultless.

Likewise, Jesus, the human lamb, was observed and tested for five days by the religious leaders. They questioned His authority (see Matthew 21:23-27). They asked Him trick questions hoping He would somehow give a wrong answer that they could use against Him (see Matthew 23). They did everything they could to point an accusing finger at Him. They wanted to discredit Him so that He would not be an acceptable sacrifice.

But Jesus always responded to them perfectly. They could not find anything wrong with Him. Finally in desperation, they took Jesus to the Roman governor, whose name was Pilate, hoping he could find something wrong with Jesus. But after interrogating and beating Jesus, Pilate said of Him, "I find no fault in Him" (John 19:4). This all happened in the five-day period from the tenth to the 14th when the Jews were checking the lambs for sacrifice. Finally, Jesus was crucified on the 14th. He was not only crucified on the same day the lambs were killed, but also at the same time of day.

With this many lambs, it was necessary for the Jews to prepare them for sacrifice at nine o'clock in the morning on the 14th. They then killed them at three o'clock that afternoon so that the Passover could be completed before six o'clock, which would begin a new day.

At the exact hour when the Jews were preparing their lambs for sacrifice, Jesus was nailed to the cross. Mark wrote, "Now it was the third hour, and they crucified Him" (Mark 15:25). The third hour was nine o'clock in the morning Jewish time.

In fulfillment of the Feast of Passover and Isaiah's prophecy, Jesus bore our griefs and carried our sorrows. He was wounded for our transgressions and bruised for our iniquities. The Lord God laid on Jesus the iniquity of us all. Jesus was oppressed, and He was afflicted. Yet He opened not His mouth, like a lamb led to the slaughter (see Isa. 53:4-7).

Then at three o'clock as the people were praising God and slaughtering the lambs, Jesus died. Mark was careful to note the time and wrote that it was the ninth hour (three o'clock Jewish time) when Jesus breathed His last breath (see Mark 15:33-37).

Jesus gave His total self to be roasted and consumed in the judgment fires of God as He died for our sins. The spit shaped like a crossbar on which the lambs were spread open pointed to Jesus hanging on the cross.

All the other details concerning the death of the lambs happened to Jesus—the real Lamb of God. For example, His bones were not broken. Remember, God said not to break any bones in the Passover lamb (see Exod. 12:46; Num. 9:12; Ps. 34:20).

When a person is crucified, his body sags so that he cannot breathe. This causes him to push himself up with his heels just long enough to take a deep breath. To hasten the person's death, a Roman soldier would break his legs; thus, he would not be able to push himself up to get air.

John records that the soldiers broke the legs of the two thieves who were crucified next to Jesus. But when they came to Jesus, they saw that He was already dead, so they did not break His legs (see John 19:30-37). John saw this and wrote, "For these things were done that the Scripture should be fulfilled, 'Not one of His bones shall be broken'" (John 19:36).

God had specifically instructed the Jews to consume the whole lamb. Nothing was to be left over for the next day (see Exod. 12:10). This also was the case with Jesus. The Jewish religious leaders, not realizing they were carrying out God's plan, hurriedly had Jesus' body taken down before six o'clock.

John wrote, "Therefore, because it was the Preparation Day, that the bodies should not remain on the cross on the Sabbath (for that Sabbath was a high day), the Jews asked Pilate that their legs might be broken, and that they might be taken away" (John 19:31). Jesus, the Sacrificial Lamb, was not left on the cross the next day but gave His all on the 14th as the final Passover sacrifice.

The blood of the Passover lamb was a visual aid and dress rehearsal directing the Jews into the future when Jesus would come and establish the spiritual reality that the lambs could only symbolize. The blood of Jesus saves us from death and gives us the promise of resurrection.

Peter wrote, "Knowing that you were not redeemed with corruptible things, like silver or gold, from your aimless conduct received by tradition from your fathers, but with the precious blood of Christ [Messiah], as of a lamb without blemish and without spot. He indeed was foreordained before the foundation of the world, but was manifest in these last times for you who through Him believe in God, who raised Him from the dead and gave Him glory, so that your faith and hope are in God" (1 Peter 1:18-21).

The apostle Paul made this connection when he said, "For indeed Christ [Messiah], our Passover, was sacrificed for us" (1 Cor. 5:7).

WHEN WAS JESUS CRUCIFIED AND RESURRECTED?

Have you ever wondered how a Friday-to-Sunday crucifixion and resurrection can be possible since the Bible says that Jesus would be in the grave for three days and three nights? Well, it is not possible. How did we get this idea? This teaching came about many centuries ago because the early Christian leaders were Gentiles who did not understand the biblical Hebraic-Jewish roots of the story.

For example, when John says that Jesus was crucified on the Preparation Day and that the body of Jesus should not remain on the cross on the Sabbath (see John 19:31), the scholars assumed John meant the weekly Saturday Sabbath. So, in their minds, Jesus must have been crucified on Friday. However, the Scripture clearly says that the Sabbath was a "High Sabbath," not the weekly Sabbath. We learn in Leviticus 23 that there was a number of "High Sabbath" days connected to the feasts that were not the weekly Sabbath.

To help clarify this understanding, please refer to the chart *When Was Jesus Crucified and Resurrected?* (page 61). Notice there are two timelines on the chart. The top timeline shows the days as reckoned on the Gentile calendar from Tuesday to Sunday beginning at midnight from April 3 to April 7. The bottom timeline shows the same information with the biblical Hebrew calendar days beginning at 6:00 P.M. as the approximate beginning of the new day (24-hour period).

One reason this timeline can be confusing is because the biblical day actually begins at night. We learn in the Book of Genesis that the evening and the morning were the first day (see Genesis 1:5). Now the Gentile calendar also begins at night (12:00 midnight), but we normally think about it beginning in the morning when the sun rises. For example, if you awaken at 6:00 A.M., the new day is already six hours old. With this in mind, let's study the chart with a biblical understanding of the events.

The Bible says that out of the mouth of two or three witnesses a thing is confirmed (see Deut. 17:6; Matt. 18:16). I want to give you four witnesses to substantiate the information presented on the chart.

The first witness is the witness of the Torah. Jesus said He came to fulfill (embody the spiritual purpose and reality of) the Torah. We discussed this in the first chapter when I explained what Jesus meant when He said, "Do not think that I came to destroy the Law or the Prophets. I did not come to destroy but to fulfill" (Matt. 5:17). In order for Jesus to be the Jewish Messiah, He had to be crucified, buried, and resurrected on feast days. As we will see on both of the charts and in the next two chapters, Jesus was crucified on the Feast of Passover (14th), buried on the Feast of Unleavened Bread (15th), and resurrected at the close of the Sabbath at the beginning of the Feast of Firstfruits (17th-18th).

Second is the witness of the sign of Jonah. Jesus told His disciples that He would be crucified on Passover to fulfill the sign of Jonah (see Matt. 12:40; 26:2). Matthew reads, "For as Jonah was three days and three nights in the belly of the great fish, so will the Son of Man be three days and three nights in the heart of the earth" (Matt. 12:40).

Jesus said three days and three nights. Whenever the Bible connects days and nights with the word "and," it means the full 24-hour period. So three days and three nights mean a 72-hour period of time. The only way that Jesus could be in the tomb for the required full three days and three nights (a 72-hour period) and fulfill the witness of the Torah is if He was crucified on Wednesday and resurrected at the close of the weekly Sabbath and the beginning of the first day of the week, the Feast of Firstfruits.

The third witness is the witness of culture. In Bible times, people believed that when people died, their spirit/soul hovered over the body for three days and three nights deciding if it wanted to depart to the next world or return to the body. This means that in the New Testament a person (Jesus, for example) was not considered fully dead until the passing of 72 hours. From a cultural understanding, Jesus had to be in the tomb for a full 72 hours. This is the reason why Jesus delayed going to Bethany when He learned that Lazarus had died.

John tells the story, "So, when He [Jesus] heard that he [Lazarus] was sick, He stayed two more days in the place where He was....So when Jesus came, He found that he [Lazarus] has already been in the tomb four days....Jesus said, 'Take away the stone.' Martha, the sister of him who was dead, said to Him, 'Lord, by this time there is a stench, for he has been dead four days'" (John 11:6,17,39).

Without understanding the cultural background to this story, we would miss the whole point of why Jesus delayed for two days, why John informs us that Lazarus had been in the tomb four days, and why Martha would say that her brother was dead. Jesus delayed so that everyone would know that Lazarus was really and truly dead. Jesus did this in order to prepare people for His own death, burial, and resurrection. He had to be in the tomb a full three days and three nights.

The fourth witness is that of astronomy. Notice I said astronomy, not astrology. With the help of computers we are able to calculate the calendar year, month, and day of historical events. When using the computer to consider possible dates for the crucifixion of Jesus, only one date is compatible with the other three witnesses. According to Edward M. Reingolds' classic work, *Calendar Book, Papers, and Code*, that date is Wednesday, April 3, in the year A.D. 30.[4] Jesus was crucified on this date and resurrected at the close of the Sabbath (Saturday P.M.) on April 6, the 17th of *Nisan*. Look at the chart as I explain the timing of the events.

Notice on the timeline that the Feast of Passover was the Preparation Day John mentioned. The Preparation Day was the preparation for the first day of the Feast of Unleavened Bread, which was the High Sabbath, a special day of rest. The Scripture that refers to this is Leviticus 23:6-7.

On the Gentile timeline this was on Wednesday, April 3, which is the 14th of *Nisan* on the Hebrew timeline. For convenience, I am repeating John's comments here, "Therefore, because it was the Preparation Day [Wednesday, Passover the 14th], that the bodies should not remain on the cross on the Sabbath (for that Sabbath [Thursday, the first day of the Feast of Unleavened Bread the 15th] was a high day), the Jews asked Pilate that their legs might be broken, and that they might be taken away" (John 19:31). According to the Scriptures, Jesus was crucified at 9:00 A.M. and died at 3:00 P.M. on Passover. (See Matthew 26-27; Mark 15; Luke 23; John 19.)

Because the next day was the High Sabbath, the Jews (that is, the High Priest) demanded that Jesus' body be taken down from the cross before sunset on the fourteenth, at roughly 6:00 P.M. So at 3:00 P.M., Joseph of Arimathea got permission from Pilate to take Jesus' body down and put it in a nearby tomb. With help from Nicodemus, they hurriedly took Jesus' body off the cross, bound it in linen strips, and anointed it with 100 pounds of spices. Then they put Jesus' body in a nearby tomb at the close of the day. Once again, the next day, which was the first day of Unleavened Bread, started at sunset. (See John 19:38-42.)

Since the High Sabbath was a special day of rest, the people could not do any ordinary work. They stayed in their homes on Thursday and rested on Friday and Saturday. Then as soon as Saturday was over, around 6:00 P.M., Mary Magdalene went to the tomb. John tells us that it was still dark when Mary got to the tomb, "Now the first day of the week Mary Magdalene went to the tomb early, while it was still dark, and saw that the stone had been taken away from the tomb" (John 20:1).

Since Jesus was already gone from the tomb when Mary got there, this can only mean that He was resurrected at sunset at the close of the weekly Sabbath and the beginning of the first day of the week, which was the Feast of Firstfruits. This was on the 17th-18th.

Once again, notice from the chart that Jesus was in the tomb on Wednesday (night 1, 6:00 P.M.–6:00 A.M.), Thursday (day 1, 6:00 A.M.–6:00 P.M.), Thursday (night 2, 6:00 P.M.–6:00 A.M.), Friday (day 2, 6:00 A.M.–6:00 P.M.), Friday (night 3, 6:00 P.M.–6:00 A.M.), and Saturday (day 3, 6:00 A.M.–6:00 P.M.). This is the exact fulfillment of the witness of the Torah, the witness of the sign of Jonah of three days and three nights, the witness of culture, and the witness of astronomy for the year A.D. 30. Hallelujah, He has risen!

WHO KILLED JESUS?

For almost 2,000 years the Church has persecuted the Jews on the basis that the Jews "killed Christ." Whenever Gentiles have suffered, they blamed their suffering on the Jews and justified persecuting them on the claim that the Jews killed God. This is called deicide. This erroneous accusation came about because the Church has misunderstood the New Testament as well as its own hatred of Jews. When we study the New Testament within its cultural context, we discover that it tells a different story.

So, who really killed Jesus? There is a theological answer and a human answer. Theologically, there are three parties involved in the death of Jesus.

God initiated the death of Jesus to provide atonement for our sins. In the passage from Isaiah quoted earlier, the prophet said: "Surely He has borne our griefs and carried our sorrows; yet we esteemed Him stricken, smitten by God, and afflicted. But He was wounded for our transgressions, He was bruised for our iniquities; the chastisement for our peace was upon Him, and by His stripes we are healed" (Isa. 53:4-5).

Notice that Isaiah says that Jesus was smitten by God. The second party to His death is Jesus Himself. Jesus willfully gave His life as the atonement for our sins. Isaiah further writes, "He was oppressed and He was afflicted, yet He opened not His mouth; He was led as a lamb to the slaughter, and as a sheep before its shearers is silent, so He opened not His mouth" (Isa. 53:7).

Jesus must have been thinking about the words of Isaiah when He said, "Therefore My Father loves Me, because I lay down My life that I may take it again. No one takes it from Me, but I lay it down of Myself. I have power to lay it down, and I have power to take it again" (John 10:17-18).

The third party who contributed to the death of Jesus is humanity. We killed Jesus because of our sins. Once again we read from Isaiah, "All we like sheep have gone astray; we have turned; everyone, to his own way: and the Lord has laid on Him the iniquity of us all" (Isa. 53:6).

Most Christians understand the theological answer to who killed Jesus. It is the human answer that has been misunderstood. There are two human parties involved in the death of Jesus. They can both be summed up in two words, "the establishment." The establishment, the people in power, always kills the prophets and revolutionaries of its day. Jesus was both a prophet and a revolutionary. He threatened their position of power, status, and wealth. So they had to get rid of Him.

The first of the two establishments responsible for the death of Jesus was Rome. By Rome I mean the government of Rome, not the people of Rome. The Roman people had never even heard of Jesus. The Roman people lived in Italy and throughout the Roman Empire. They certainly didn't live in Israel where Jesus lived and died. Even though the Roman government in Israel crucified Jesus by the hands of Pilate and a few Roman soldiers, we cannot hold the Roman people responsible for the death of Jesus. Modern Italians did not kill Jesus. They were not part of the crowd in Jerusalem shouting, "Crucify Him." (See Luke 23:21.)

The New Testament is clear that Pilate took it upon himself to put Jesus to death. Luke reads, "So Pilate gave sentence that it should be as they requested" (Luke 23:24).

The second human establishment that killed Jesus was Jerusalem. By Jerusalem I mean the Jewish religious and political leaders in Jerusalem. As a citizen of the United States, I often use the word "Washington" to speak of the political center of the United States. When I say "Washington," I am not referring to the American people but to the American government. Likewise, when the New Testament says that the "Jews" killed Jesus, it is not referring to the ordinary Jew who lived in Israel and Jerusalem. It is referring to the Jewish political and religious leaders over the Jewish people—that is, the Jewish government operating under Roman rule.

In the time of Jesus, there were over 20 Jewish sects in Israel. They all had different views about the Messiah and constantly argued among themselves. There was not "one voice" that spoke for the Jews. Jews who lived in the north were called "Galileans." They were hardworking country folk who talked with a country twang. Peter's Galilean accent gave him away as a disciple of Jesus (see Luke 22:59). The establishment in Jerusalem considered the Galileans uncultured and unsophisticated.

The Jews who lived in the south were called "Judeans." There was no love lost between the Galileans in the north and the Judeans in the south. The Judeans were more cosmopolitan than the Galileans. They considered themselves to be highbred, sophisticated, and cultured. They were well-educated and looked down their noses at the Galileans.

When the New Testament talks about the Jews killing Jesus, it is referring to the Judeans, specifically the Jewish establishment in Jerusalem who owed their allegiance, position, power, and influence to the Romans. While there were some influential Pharisees at the highest level, the Jewish establishment consisted primarily of the Sadducees.

The Sadducees represented a very small group of powerful religious leaders. They were the priests who oversaw the activities at the temple and greatly profited from the merchandising at the temple. This group desired to crucify Jesus because they were jealous of His fame and were afraid He would upset their comfortable relationship with the Roman government ruling over them. It was really just a small group of the ruling elite. Matthew 27:18 says that Pilate knew that the Sadducees handed Jesus over to him because they were envious of Jesus. The high priest and his followers handed Jesus over to Pilate because it was the "politically correct" thing for them to do.

John 11 reads, "Then the chief priests and the Pharisees gathered a council and said, 'What shall we do? For this man works many signs. If we let Him alone like this, everyone will believe in Him, and the Romans will come and take away both our place and our nation.' And one of them, Caiaphas, being the high priest that year, said to them, 'You know nothing at all, nor do you understand that it is expedient for us that one man should die for the people, and not that the whole nation should perish'" (John 11:47-50).

When the high priest had Jesus arrested at night, the ordinary Jerusalemites were in their homes preparing for Passover meals and sleeping. They did not know what was happening. They would have surely protested because many of them believed in Jesus. In fact, Jesus had so many followers in Jerusalem that the Sadducees had to wait until night to arrest Jesus for fear of an uproar by the people.

Matthew writes, "You know that after two days is the Passover, and the Son of Man will be delivered up to be crucified." Then the chief priests, the scribes, and the elders of the people assembled at the palace of the high priest, who was called Caiaphas, and plotted to take Jesus by trickery and kill Him. But they said, "Not during the feast, lest there be an uproar among the people" (Matt. 26:2-5).

The high priest did what politicians do today. He rented a crowd. He instructed and coerced his own followers, all with a vested interest in the status quo, to get a crowd and assemble them. Matthew writes, "But the chief priests and elders persuaded the multitudes that they should ask for Barabbas and destroy Jesus" (Matt. 27:20). At the right moment, they were instructed to cry out, "Give us Barabbas, crucify Jesus" (see Matt. 27:21-22).

This was a completely different crowd of people than those who earlier greeted and cheered Jesus when He rode into Jerusalem. Their response to Him was, "...Hosanna to the Son of David! Blessed is He who comes in the name of the Lord! Hosanna in the highest!" (Matt. 21:9).

When Pilate pretended to absolve himself from being responsible for the death of Jesus, the "rent-a-crowd" said, "...His blood be on us and our children" (Matt. 27:25). Because of this statement, Church leaders have erroneously believed that the Jews, as a collective group of people, pronounced a curse on themselves forever. Therefore, they are the "Christ killers."

But as we have just learned, this was the Sadducees and a small mob crowd they assembled in order to influence Pilate. Their self-curse was fulfilled 40 years later when Titus burned the temple and destroyed Jerusalem. Since the Sadducees were the priests administering the temple, they and their families and their power, position, privilege, and fortune came to an end.

Most Jews did not live in Israel during the time of Jesus. They were scattered throughout the Roman Empire. They had never heard of Jesus, so they were certainly not guilty of killing Him. Furthermore, as we have just read, most of the Jews in Jerusalem believed in Jesus; they certainly didn't kill Him.

Jesus suffered and died for our sins. God could have used any ethnic group to carry out the execution. In His redemptive plans and purposes and time, it was a petty Roman bureaucrat and a small handful of priests who actually put Jesus to death.

Christians should continuously thank God for His redemptive love demonstrated through the death of Jesus as our Passover Lamb. We should also ask forgiveness from our Jewish friends for blaming them for His death.

PERSONAL APPLICATION

Let's now look at the personal application this feast has for us today. The Bible says and the human condition proves that all of us have sinned and that the judgment for our sin is death (see Rom. 3:23; 6:23). As with the Hebrews back in Egypt, the angel of death comes knocking at our door. The writer of Hebrews tells us that the great hold that satan has on humanity is the fear of death (see Heb. 2:14-15). Death is the one subject we don't like to think of or talk about.

Not only are we afraid of death, but we are also afraid of God. We are afraid of God because deep down inside we know we are sinners and that our sins have separated us from God. We know that God would be perfectly just in punishing us. So we run from God. We try to hide from Him behind the walls of religion, business, power, money, fame, glamour, success, etc. We keep ourselves busy and numb our minds in order not to think about Him. The prophet Isaiah observed this in humans and wrote, "'there is no peace for the wicked,' says the Lord" (Isa. 48:22).

Even though we deserve death, God has made a way for us to be saved. That way is through the blood of Jesus, which cleanses us from all sin (see 1 John 1:7). When we apply His blood to the doorpost of our heart, death cannot hold us. We no longer need to fear death because the resurrection of Jesus has taken away its sting (see 1 Cor. 15:51-57).

The same is true of our fear of God. We no longer have to run from God when we accept Jesus as the Lamb of God who died for our sins. God accepts Jesus' death in our place. He is our innocent substitutionary sacrifice. We are reconciled to God when we acknowledge Jesus as the one who died on our behalf.

Paul wrote, "But now in Christ Jesus [Messiah Yeshua] you who once were far off have been brought near by the blood of Christ [Messiah]" (Eph. 2:13). This means there is no condemnation for those who come to Jesus and receive Him as Messiah, Lord, and Savior (see Romans 8:1). We shall not come into condemnation, for we have passed from death to life (see John 5:24).

The result of our coming to Jesus as our Passover sacrifice is peace with God. We read these words in Romans, "Therefore, having been justified by faith, we have peace with God through our Lord Jesus Christ [Yeshua the Messiah]...But God demonstrates His own love toward us, in that while we were still sinners, Christ [Messiah] died for us. Much more then, having now been justified by His blood, we shall be saved from the wrath of God through Him" (Rom. 5:1,8-9).

Our Father in Heaven has offered the blood of His own Son as the Passover-threshold covenant sacrifice. By embracing Jesus as our Passover Lamb, God has entered our house—that is, our life. He has become our protector and provider. We have crossed over from being natural people to covenant people, from darkness to light, from sin to righteousness, from bondage to liberty, from defeat to victory, from fear to faith, from sickness to health, from poverty to plenty, and from death to life. Therefore, let us not trample under our feet the sacred threshold-blood covenant God has made for us through Jesus and treat it as a common thing. But let us hold fast the confession of our hope without wavering, for our God is a faithful, covenant-keeping God. (See Hebrews 10.)

Accepting Jesus as our Messiah, Lord, and Savior is the first major encounter we have with God. This is how we find peace with God. This is what the Feast of Passover symbolizes. It is the picture of the Prince of Peace, the Lord Jesus.

The first of the seven steps to know God and walk with Him is to accept Jesus as our personal Messiah, Lord, and Savior and thereby experience a spiritual new birth.

God told the Hebrews that no uncircumcised person could celebrate the Passover feast or the Passover meal (see Exod. 12:48). As I pointed out earlier, circumcision was the outward evidence that the person was in covenant with God. If a person accepted circumcision, it showed that he recognized the God of Abraham, Isaac, and Jacob as his own God. This enabled him to receive the blessings that were part of God's covenant with the Jewish people.

But God was interested in something much greater than just a cutting of the flesh. He wanted the people to have a circumcised heart (see Rom. 2:29). Jesus spoke of this as being "born again" (John 3:1-7). This is a spiritual rebirth that takes place the moment we accept Jesus as our Passover Lamb and ask Him to come into our life. Jesus gives us the Holy Spirit who comes to live in us, changing our heart and making us a new creation in spiritual union with Jesus. This is what God had always intended for His people. Physical circumcision was just a picture of the true circumcision, which was of the Spirit and in the heart.

Paul often contrasted physical and spiritual circumcision to point out the inadequacy of the physical and the necessity of the spiritual. He said, "For we are the circumcision, who worship God in the Spirit, rejoice in Christ Jesus [Messiah Yeshua], and have no confidence in the flesh" (Phil. 3:3).

Paul further wrote to his Jewish brethren, "For he is not a Jew who is one outwardly, nor is circumcision that which is outward in the flesh; but he is a Jew who is one inwardly, and circumcision is that of the heart, in the Spirit" (Rom. 2:28-29). Paul did not mean that a natural-born Jew was not a Jew. He meant that a natural-born Jew must also be born of the Spirit.

He goes on to say, "For in Christ Jesus [Messiah Yeshua] neither circumcision nor uncircumcision avails anything, but a new creation" (Gal. 6:15). And to the believers in Corinth, Paul wrote, "Therefore, if anyone is in Christ [Messiah], he is a new creation; old things have passed away; behold, all things have become new" (2 Cor. 5:17).

PROPHETIC SEASONAL ASPECT

We've learned from the Book of Leviticus that the Lord told His people to keep the feasts in their seasons (see Lev. 23:4). By this He meant the agricultural seasons. God also has prophetic seasons. God's prophetic seasons are those periods of time in world history when God moves to establish and restore the spiritual meanings of these feasts in the lives of His covenant people. These are major moves of God that affect the whole world, but particularly Jews and Christians.

You'll notice from the Feasts chart that the seasonal aspect of Passover is connected with Martin Luther. Here's what happened. For centuries, the biblical truth pictured by the Feast of Passover was not clearly taught by the religious leaders of the Church. This came about in the following way.

In A.D. 312, the Roman Emperor Constantine decreed that Christianity was to be the official religion of the Roman Empire. Of course no one can decree that another person become a Christian. Christianity is a matter of the heart. But the people had to outwardly obey even though inwardly most never actually accepted Jesus personally and experienced a new birth. Rome embraced Christianity, but the Romans themselves did not become true believers. In order to survive and advance in the empire, the people joined a new religion, but they never had a change on the inside.

During the next 1,200 years, many unbiblical practices were taught by the institutional Church. The church lost the simple teaching of justification by faith and faith alone. People sought salvation through religious rituals rather than personal faith in Jesus as their human Passover Lamb.

Many of the Church leaders themselves had not experienced their own spiritual birth. As a result they did not clearly teach that salvation came about through a personal relationship with Jesus and a spiritual new birth into the Kingdom of God. Over time, the common person did not hear or understand the significance of the Feast of Passover as fulfilled in Jesus. People sought salvation through Church rituals rather than through personal faith in Jesus as their human Passover Lamb.

In the 1500s, God raised up a man named Martin Luther to restore the meaning of the Feast of Passover to the Christian world. At the age of 22, during a terrible thunderstorm, Luther was knocked to the ground by a bolt of lightning. Because his life was spared, Luther made a vow to become a monk. He was ordained in 1507, and after studying theology, he taught religion at the University of Wittenberg.

Because of his theological orientation, Luther sought peace with God through all the rituals and traditions of the Church. He kept them all, as best a man could, with great zeal and devotion. He fasted, he prayed, he confessed his sins, he appealed to the saints and the Virgin Mary for help. He forsook all creature comforts and submitted his body to the most primitive conditions in an attempt to gain favor with God and overcome temptation. His failures to find peace with God through these outward works left him empty, confused, and frustrated. In the context of this book, we would say Luther was focusing on the pictures rather than the person.

In the year 1515, Luther devoted himself to studying Paul's letter to the Romans. It was during this study that Luther came to realize that salvation was not based on religious acts or outward works, but was a free gift from God available through personal faith in Jesus. The particular verse that God used to open Luther's eyes was Romans 1:17 which says, "...the just shall live by faith."

With this fresh understanding of God's Word, Luther became a changed man. He put his personal faith in Jesus as his Passover Lamb who had died for his sins. The whole of Scripture took on new meaning for Luther. He proclaimed his new understanding with a boldness that shook the world.

Unfortunately, Martin Luther hated Jews. He was a man of his times and lived in an anti-Semitic world. Yet, God used him to restore the spiritual reality of the Feast of Passover as it was fulfilled in Jesus. In 1517, Luther protested the Church's sale of indulgences, which triggered the Protestant Reformation that changed the course of history.

PERSONAL STUDY REVIEW

1. Describe how Jesus fulfilled the Feast of Passover.

2. How does the Feast of Passover apply to our lives today?

3. Describe the seasonal aspect of the Feast of Passover.

4. Ask God to give you a personal encounter with Jesus as the spiritual reality of this feast.

ENDNOTES

1. "Strong's #6452, Pâsach," StudyLight.org, accessed July 01, 2015, http://www.studylight.org/lexicons/hebrew/hwview.cgi ?n=06452.

2. For a description of how Passover was celebrated in the first century, see Daniel B. Wallace, "Passover in the Time of Jesus," Bible.org, May 28, 2004, https://bible.org/article/ passover-time-jesus.

3. Josephus, *The Wars of the Jews in The Works of Josephus* (Peabody, MA: Hendrickson, 1980).

4. See Edward M. Reingold, *Calendar Book, Papers, and Code, Calendrical Calculations,* Third Edition (Cambridge: Cambridge University Press, 2008).

The Feasts of the Lord

Farming Season	Hebrew Month	Feast (Historical)	Jesus (Prophetic)	Believer (Personal)	Seasonal
Barley Harvest	Nisan	**Passover**			
	14	Passover	Crucified	New Birth	Luther-1517
	15-21	Unleavened Bread	Buried	Put Off Old	Luther-1517
	17-18	Firstfruits	Resurrected	Put On New	Wesley-1738
	Iyyar	50 Days From Resurrection To Pentecost			
Wheat Harvest	Sivan	**Pentecost**	Exalted	Baptism In Holy Spirit	Kansas-1901 Los An.-1906
	6				
Fruit Harvest	Tammuz	No Feast—The Church Period			
	Ab				
	Elul				
Final Ingathering	Tishri	**Tabernacles**			
	1	Trumpets	Defeating Enemy	Full Armor	Present
	10	Day of Aton	Purifying Bride	Baptism In Fire	Future
	15-21	Tabernacles	Coming Again	God's Rest	Future

Nisan—Mar-Apr
Iyyar—Apr-May
Sivan—May-Jun
Tammu—Jun-Jul
Ab—Jul-Aug
Elul—Aug-Sept
Tishri—Sept-Oct

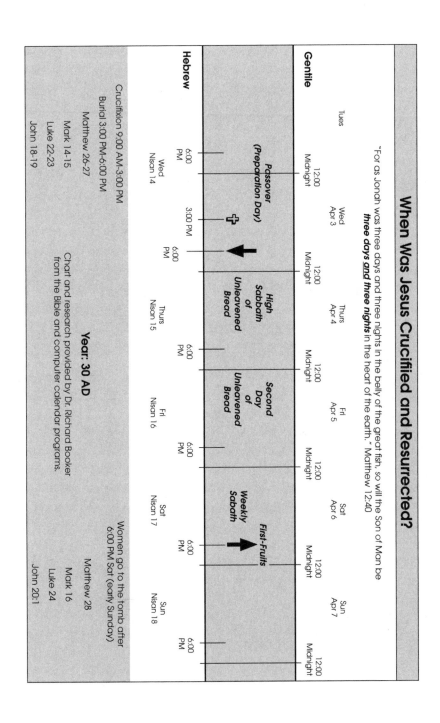

When Was Jesus Crucified and Resurrected?

"For as Jonah was three days and three nights in the belly of the great fish, so will the Son of Man be *three days and three nights* in the heart of the earth." Matthew 12:40

Year: 30 AD

Chart and research provided by Dr. Richard Booker from the Bible and computer calendar programs.

CHAPTER 3

UNLEAVENED BREAD

The Feast of Passover as fulfilled in Jesus affects your position before God. Prior to receiving Jesus as your Messiah, Lord, and Savior, your sins separate you from God. But once you accept Jesus as the Passover Lamb of God who died for your sins, your position before God changes. Something wonderful happens! God declares you "not guilty."

This change in your position before God is called justification. It is a judicial act of God regarding your position before Him. In justifying you, God imputes or credits the perfect righteousness of Jesus to your spiritual bank account. The following Scriptures speak of this wonderful blessing from God.

> "...being justified freely by His grace through the redemption that is in Christ Jesus [Messiah Yeshua].... Therefore we conclude that a man is justified by faith apart from the deeds of the law" (Romans. 3:24,28).

> "But to him who does not work but believes on Him who justifies the ungodly, his faith is accounted for

righteousness, just as David also describes the blessedness of the man to whom God imputes righteousness apart from works: 'Blessed are those whose lawless deeds are forgiven, and whose sins are covered; Blessed is the man to whom the Lord shall not impute sin'" (Romans 4:5-8).

"Therefore, having been justified by faith, we have peace with God through our Lord Jesus Christ [Yeshua the Messiah]. But God demonstrates His own love toward us, in that while we were still sinners, Christ [Messiah] died for us. Much more then, having now been justified by His blood, we shall be saved from wrath through Him" (Romans 5:1;8-9).

"Knowing that a man is not justified by the works of the law but by faith in Jesus Christ [Yeshua the Messiah], even we have believed in Christ [Messiah], that we might be justified by faith in Christ [Messiah] and not by the works of the law; for by the works of the law no flesh shall be justified" (Galatians 2:16).

Paul was referring to our justification when he wrote, "For He [God] made Him [Jesus] who knew no sin to be sin for us, that we might become the righteousness of God in Him" (2 Cor. 5:21).

God declares us to be righteous through Jesus. This is great news and cause for rejoicing. We are no longer running from God, carrying the burden of guilt through sin. God has forgiven our sins. He doesn't even remember them. He has separated us from our sins as far as the east is from the west. He has cast them into the sea of forgetfulness. We have peace with God. Wow! May His name be praised forever!

Many Christians think this is all God has for them. But there is much more! This is just the beginning of an exciting walk with God.

You see, God is not only interested in our position; He is also interested in our condition. God not only cares about what we were and what we are going to be; He also cares about what we are now. God is interested in every part of our life. He wants to change our life and transform us into the moral image and character of Jesus. And He wants to do it now! This is the spiritual teaching of the Feast of Unleavened Bread.

HISTORICAL BACKGROUND

God gives the following instructions concerning the Feast of Unleavened Bread, "And on the fifteenth day of the same month is the Feast of Unleavened Bread to the Lord; seven days you must eat unleavened bread. On the first day you shall have a holy convocation; you shall do no customary work on it. But you shall offer an offering made by fire to the Lord for seven days. The seventh day shall be a holy convocation; you shall do no customary work on it" (Lev. 23:6-8).

We notice from this Scripture that the first and last days of this feast (the 15th and 21st) are High Sabbath days. On these days, the people were to cease from their labors and spend time meditating on God and His greatness and goodness. The 15th is the High Sabbath we discussed in the previous chapter that is referred to in John 19:31. Passover, the 14th, was the Preparation Day for the first day of the Feast of Unleavened Bread, the 15th. We also learn from the Book of Numbers that sacrifices were offered to God during this feast (see Num. 28:16-25).

The Feast of Unleavened Bread was celebrated the day after Passover and lasted from the 15th to the 21st in the Hebrew month of Nisan. This is in the spring months of March-April on the Gentile calendar.

When God delivered the Hebrews from Egypt, He brought them out with such haste that they did not have time to bake their bread, which would have normally included leaven. Over time, leaven became symbolic of the Hebrew's old life of bondage in Egypt under Pharaoh and the Egyptian's world system, which was contrary to God. Unleavened bread symbolized their putting off this old life as they came out of Egypt.

God instructed the Hebrews to keep the Feast of Unleavened Bread as a memorial to their separation from Egypt. Leavened bread was not eaten at Passover on the 14th nor for the next seven days, as is stated in Exodus 13:3,7:

> *"Remember this day in which you went out of Egypt, out of the house of bondage; for by strength of hand the Lord brought you out of this place. No leavened bread shall be eaten....Unleavened bread shall be eaten seven days. And no leavened bread shall be seen among you, nor shall leaven be seen among you in all your quarters."*

Before the Feasts of Passover and Unleavened Bread could be celebrated, all the leaven was to be removed from the Hebrews' houses. This required a great amount of spring housecleaning. Everything in the house was thoroughly washed, scrubbed, and cleaned. This included the walls, ceilings, floors, furniture, cabinets, etc. The cooking ware was boiled in water, and special utensils were used that had not been contaminated with leaven.

Once the cleaning was complete, the family would participate in a ceremony called the "search for the leaven." After dark, the head of the house would take a lighted candle and diligently search through every nook and cranny of the house looking for any hidden leaven. If he found any, he would immediately remove it from the house.

Many modern Jewish families participate in this same housecleaning and search for the leaven. Just before Passover, crumbs of leavened bread are placed in each room of the house by one member of the family. Then the head of the home pronounces a benediction about removing leaven and proceeds to search for the hidden leaven. A family member goes along carrying a lighted candle to expose where the leaven is hidden. When the searcher discovers the leaven, he is careful not to touch it. To avoid contact, he takes a feather and brushes the leaven into a small wooden spoon. He then puts the leaven into a bag. When he is satisfied that he has found all the leaven, he puts the wooden spoon, the feather, and the candle into the bag and burns it. Finally, he says a prayer asking God to forgive the family for any hidden leaven they may have overlooked. With the leaven now purged from the household, the family is ready to celebrate Passover and Unleavened Bread.[1]

We can clearly see from this feast that its purpose was, and still is today, a reminder to the Jewish people that God called them out of Egypt to be a separate people unto Himself. It was a permanent memorial of their deliverance from Egypt and the bondage, oppression, sorrow, and suffering that was part of their old life.

HOW JESUS FULFILLED THE FEAST

As we've learned, the Jews were to keep this feast with unleavened bread. In later times, the rabbis added the rule that food could only be eaten during this feast if the food was cooked before the leavening process even began. It was determined that it took 18 minutes from the time the wheat is mixed with water until the time the yeast in the wheat begins to ferment.

The baking of the Passover *matzah* requires close supervision in order to meet the rigid requirements of the rabbis. Anyone who has eaten this specially prepared unleavened "bread of affliction" can't help but notice that it is bruised, striped, and pierced. The connection to Jesus is obvious.

Jesus fulfilled this feast as the "Bread of Life" from Heaven who had no leaven (sin) in Him. Because of the fermenting and permeating nature of leaven, it is often used as a metaphor for sin. There was no leaven of sin in Jesus.

Paul wrote, "For He made Him who knew no sin to be sin for us, that we might become the righteousness of God in Him" (2 Cor. 5:21).

John declared, "And you know that He was manifested to take away our sins, and in Him there is no sin" (1 John 3:5).

The prophet Isaiah gave us a preview of the Messiah who would be smitten, bruised, and pierced for our sins. We read his words in the previous chapter, but it is appropriate to read them again,

> *"Surely He has born our griefs and carried our sorrows; yet we esteemed Him stricken, smitten by God, and afflicted. But He was wounded for our transgressions, He was bruised for our iniquities; the chastisement for our peace was upon Him, and by His stripes we are healed....For the transgressions of My people He was stricken. And they made His grave with the wicked— but with the rich at His death, because He had done no violence, nor was any deceit in His mouth. Yet it pleased the Lord to bruise Him"* (Isaiah 53:4-5; 8-10).

Jesus pointed to Himself as the fulfillment of this feast the very week it was being celebrated in Jerusalem. Many Jews had come to Jerusalem to celebrate the feast according to God's command in Exodus 23:14-17 and Deuteronomy 16:16.

A huge crowd of these pilgrims had heard about Jesus and were following Him wherever He went. But a problem developed. The crowd was hungry, and there was nothing to eat. Jesus took this opportunity to perform a miracle that would point the people to Himself as the true bread of life.

Jesus used this opportunity to test His disciples. He asked Philip how they could feed all the hungry people. Philip had no ideas. Then another disciple, Andrew, brought a young boy to Jesus who had five loaves of barley and two fish. (This was during the barley harvest, and barley was the bread of the poor. The poor lad was willing to give all that he had to Jesus.) This was clearly an inadequate solution to the problem. However, Jesus took the boy's lunch, blessed His heavenly Father for the food, and then multiplied it so that there was enough to feed 5,000 men, plus the women and children, and have some left over (see John 6:1-13).

Jesus then used this miracle as a sign to tell the people of their need to come to Him as the true bread of God who would give them eternal life. John was an eyewitness and gave the following account:

> *"Then Jesus said to them, 'Most assuredly I say to you, Moses did not give you the bread from heaven, but My Father gives you the true bread from heaven. For the bread of God is He who comes down from heaven, and gives life to the world.' Then they said to Him, 'Lord, give us this bread always.' And Jesus said to them, 'I am the bread of life. He who comes to Me shall never hunger, and he who believes in Me shall never thirst'"* (John 6:32-35).

When the people heard Jesus speak, they murmured against Him. However, Jesus would not back down from His claims. He repeated Himself with great boldness and clarity:

> *"Most assuredly, I say to you, he who believes in Me has everlasting life. I am the bread of life. Your fathers ate the manna in the wilderness and are dead....I am the living bread which came down from heaven. If anyone eats of this bread, he will live forever; and the bread that I shall give is My flesh, which I shall give for the life of the world"* (John 6:47-51).

The people murmured again and argued among themselves over Jesus' sayings. Once again, Jesus pressed His point as John recorded:

*"Most assuredly, I say to you, unless you eat the flesh
of the Son of Man and drink His blood, you have
no life in you. Whoever eats My flesh and drinks My
blood has eternal life, and I will raise him up at the
last day. For My flesh is food indeed, and My blood
is drink indeed. He who eats My flesh and drinks My
blood abides in Me, and I in him. As the living Father
sent Me, and I live because of the Father, so he who
feeds on Me will live because of Me. This is the bread
which came down from heaven—not as your fathers
ate the manna, and are dead. He who eats this bread
will live forever"* (John 6:53-58).

In the previous chapter, we learned that Jesus was crucified on
the 14th, a Wednesday. (Refer to the chart When Was Jesus Crucified and Resurrected?) We also noted that His body was taken down
just before six o'clock that evening, which would begin the next day
(the 15th). From this we realize that Joseph of Arimathea and Nicodemus prepared Jesus' body for burial and placed Him in Joseph's
tomb just in time for Jesus to be buried on the 15th, which was the
first day of the Feast of Unleavened Bread.

Jesus, the unleavened bread of God from Heaven, took on all
our leaven of sin and was buried on the same day the Jews had been
celebrating the feast for centuries. What the Jews had been portray-
ing in the Feast of Unleavened Bread was a visual aid pointing them
to Messiah Jesus who had come and fulfilled in His flesh the reality
pictured by the feast. While the Jewish people were removing the
physical leaven from their houses, Jesus removed the spiritual leaven
of sin from our house—that is, our life.

Jesus took our leaven of sin in His spirit, our leaven of sorrows in
His soul, and our leaven of sickness, disease, and death in His body.
He who knew no leaven (sin, sickness, and death) became leaven for
us. Our worldly attitudes and sinful ways were buried with Him.

The bondage, oppression, sorrow, and suffering that were part of our old life went with Him into the grave. He took the full burden of all the liabilities of our human condition with Him.

Joseph of Arimathea and Nicodemus were important members of the Jewish Supreme Court (the Sanhedrin). They took Jesus' body and wrapped it in linen bands with a mixture of myrrh and aloes weighing about 100 pounds. The amount of spices used to anoint the body was a measure of the value of the deceased. Rabbi Gamaliel was a contemporary of Jesus. When he died, his body was anointed with eighty pounds of spices.[2]

It was the custom for the body to be washed and straightened, and then bandaged tightly from the armpits to the ankles in strips of linen about a foot wide. Aromatic spices, often of a gummy consistency, were placed between the wrappings. They served partially as a preservative and partially as a cement to glue the cloth wrappings into a solid covering. The face was left uncovered, but a cloth was wrapped around the head of the dead body.

Aloe was a fragrant wood that had been pounded or in some other way reduced to dust. The myrrh was an aromatic gum that was mixed with the powdered wood. We might think of myrrh as the "first-century superglue." When mixed together, the dry aloe would stick to the body so that Jesus' body was embedded in the powdered spice.[3]

The body lay with its face turned upwards and its hands folded on the chest. The face, neck, and upper shoulders were left bare. The head would have rested on a raised portion of the ledge, which served as a pillow. Because Jesus' body was hurriedly prepared for the tomb, there was no time for an elaborate burial. Later, after the weekly Sabbath, the women would come to anoint His face, neck, and shoulders.

Before He was crucified, Jesus was beaten so badly one could hardly recognize Him as a man (see Isa. 52:14). He hung on the cross for six hours, bearing the consequences of our sins. He was wrapped up like a mummy and covered with 100 pounds of spices. Then Joseph rolled a large stone in front of the tomb (see Matt. 27:59-60). Some ancient writings say this stone was so large that it would take at least twenty men to roll it away. Finally, the tomb was secured by stretching a cord across the stone and sealed at each end with a Roman seal. Jesus lay inside with our sins, sorrows, sicknesses, and diseases buried with Him. This is how Jesus fulfilled (was the spiritual reality and human embodiment of) the Feast of Unleavened Bread.

PERSONAL APPLICATION

Paul wrote that we believers are to "put off" the old leaven of sin that was crucified and buried with Jesus. We read, "That you put off, concerning your former conduct, the old man which grows corrupt according to the deceitful lusts" (Eph. 4:22).

The old nature or old man that Paul is speaking of is what the Jews call our "evil impulse." Christianity speaks of it as a sin nature inherited from Adam. This impulse or inclination toward sin keeps us from having an intimate relationship with God, brings sorrow and heartache to our soul, and brings disease and death to our body. As we can all attest, this old nature within us loves to sin. As long as it is the ruling force in our life, we will commit outward acts of sin.

Jesus said it this way, "For from within, out of the heart of men, proceed evil thoughts, adulteries, fornications, murders, thefts, covetousness, wickedness, deceit, lewdness, an evil eye, blasphemy, pride, foolishness. All these evil things come from within and defile a man" (Mark 7:21-23). Jesus took this desire to sin with Him into the tomb.

When Paul used the phrase "put off," he was referring to a person taking off his or her garment. In Bible times, a person's garment could represent the person. Today we say, "The clothes make the man (or woman)." Paul wants us to put off the "Lazarus grave clothes of the flesh," which he describes in Galatians as the works of the flesh:

> *"Now the works of the flesh are evident, which are: adultery, fornication, uncleanness, lewdness, idolatry, sorcery, hatred, contentions, jealousies, outbursts of wrath, selfish ambitions, dissensions, heresies, envy, murders, drunkenness, revelries, and the like; of which I tell you beforehand, just as I also told you in time past, that those who practice such things will not inherit the kingdom of God"* (Galatians 5:19-21).

We are able to put off this old garment of the flesh because the old man of sin was buried with Jesus in fulfillment of the Feast of Unleavened Bread. In this way, the power of sin over us has been broken. When we realize and understand this work of Jesus on our behalf, God begins to work changes in our life. He changes our condition. He changes our character. We are transformed more and more into the moral image and likeness of Jesus. This is how the Feast of Unleavened Bread as fulfilled in Jesus affects our moral and spiritual condition.

God gave the Feast of Unleavened Bread as a visual aid or picture showing the Hebrews they were to be separate from Egypt. In the Bible, Egypt represents the world system in which we live. Its philosophies and ways are contrary to the Word of God. The Hebrews were to live differently once they were delivered from Egypt. Likewise, we who have been delivered from the world system through the blood of Jesus are to live a life separated from the attitudes and ways of the world.

God has chosen us to be a people set apart and different from those around us. We are to be in the world but not of the world. This is the biblical meaning of the word "holy."

Paul expressed it this way to the Roman believers, "I beseech you therefore, brethren, by the mercies of God, that you present your bodies a living sacrifice, holy, acceptable to God, which is your reasonable service. And do not be conformed to this world, but be transformed by the renewing of your mind, that you may prove what is that good and acceptable and perfect will of God" (Rom. 12:1-2).

John wrote, "Do not love the world or the things in the world. If anyone loves the world, the love of the Father is not in him. For all that is in the world—the lust of the flesh, the lust of the eyes, and the pride of life—is not of the Father but is of the world. And the world is passing away, and the lust of it; but he who does the will of God abides forever" (1 John 2:15-17).

Peter said, "Beloved, I beg you as sojourners and pilgrims, abstain from fleshly lusts which war against the soul" (1 Pet. 2:11).

Paul instructed the believers at Corinth, "Therefore 'Come out from among them and be separate, says the Lord'" (2 Cor. 6:17).

The Feasts of Unleavened Bread and Firstfruits represent the work of God in us by His Spirit that enables us to live this holy or separate life. The Bible calls this transforming work in God in us "sanctification." (See First Thessalonians 4:3-4; Second Thessalonians 2:13; First Peter 1:2.) This is a cooperative walk with God whereby we allow Him to change us into the moral and spiritual likeness of Jesus.

Paul expressed this process in these words: "...work out your own salvation with fear and trembling; for it is God who works in you both to will and to do for His good pleasure" (Phil. 2:12-13).

The Feast of Passover is the first step in our walk with God. It relates to our position of justification. The Feasts of Unleavened Bread and Firstfruits symbolize our next two steps. They relate to our condition of sanctification, which transforms our character. This transformation results in the fruit of God's Spirit manifested in our lives. This spiritual work can be a reality in our lives because Jesus is the true unleavened Bread of God who took the leaven of our sins with Him to the grave.

PROPHETIC SEASONAL ASPECT

You will notice from the Feasts chart that the Feast of Unleavened Bread and the Feast of Firstfruits are connected with John and Charles Wesley. We learned in the previous chapter how God raised up Martin Luther in the 1500s for the purpose of restoring the spiritual significance of the Feast of Passover. Since this is the beginning step in our spiritual journey, God restored it first.

God then worked through John and Charles Wesley to restore the spiritual significance of the Feasts of Unleavened Bread and Firstfruits. While Passover relates to our position before God, these two feasts relate to our condition—that is, our character. God would use the Wesleys to show us that there is much more to being a Christian than just having our sins forgiven.

John and Charles Wesley were born in England to devoutly religious parents. John was born in 1703 and Charles in 1707. They both attended Oxford University, where Charles started what became known as the "holy club." This was a small gathering of like-minded men who desired to live a disciplined life for the purpose of developing inward holiness.

John soon became the leader of the group. As he meditated on God's Word, John began to see that "true religion was seated in the heart, and that God's law extended to all our thoughts, as well as to our words and actions."[4]

This insight became a spiritual reality in John Wesley's own life on May 24, 1738, while he was attending a Christian gathering on Aldersgate Street in London. When the minister read Martin Luther's comments on Paul's letter to the Romans, John felt his heart "strangely warmed" by the Spirit of God. Charles had a similar experience three days later.

This personal encounter with the living Lord totally transformed the Wesleys. Their preaching focused on the necessity for personal holiness in the lives of those who professed Jesus as Lord and Savior. During their ministry, John rode over 250,000 miles proclaiming the Word of God, and Charles wrote more than 6,000 hymns, poems, and spiritual songs. This restoration of the prophetic season of the Feasts of Unleavened Bread and Firstfruits would have a major impact on the world.

PERSONAL STUDY REVIEW

1. Describe how Jesus fulfilled the Feast of Unleavened Bread.

2. How does the Feast of Unleavened Bread as revealed in Jesus apply to our lives today?

3. Describe the seasonal aspect of the Feast of Unleavened Bread.

4. Ask God to give you a personal encounter with Jesus as the spiritual reality of this feast.

ENDNOTES

1. "Leaven," JewishEncyclopedia.com, Search for Leaven Before Passover, accessed July 01, 2015, http://www.jewishencyclopedia.com/articles/9694-leaven.

2. William Anderson Scott, The Christ of the Apostles' Creed (New York: A.D.F. Randolph, 1867).

3. On first-century burial customs, see, for example, Craig A. Evans, "Jewish Burial Traditions and the Resurrection of Jesus" (thesis, Acadia Divinity College), accessed July 1, 2015, www.craigaevans.com/Burial_Traditions.pdf.

4. Nehemiah Curnock, ed., *The Journal of the Rev. John Wesley*, A. M. (New York: Eaton and Maine, 1909), I, 466.

CHAPTER 4

FIRSTFRUITS

The third step in our walk with God is represented by the Feast of Firstfruits. As with the Feast of Unleavened Bread, it too relates to our condition as believers in and followers of Jesus. These feasts show the two different phases of Christian commitment that are necessary to change our spiritual condition. These two phases are separation and consecration. Whereas the Feast of Unleavened Bread teaches us about separation, the Feast of Firstfruits teaches us about consecration.

HISTORICAL BACKGROUND

God gives the following instructions concerning this feast:

> "And the Lord spoke to Moses saying, 'Speak to the children of Israel, and say to them: "When you come into the land which I give to you, and reap its harvest, then you shall bring a sheaf of the firstfruits of your harvest to the priest. He shall wave the sheaf before the Lord, to be accepted on your behalf....And you shall

offer on that day, when you wave the sheaf, a male lamb of the first year, without blemish, as a burnt offering to the Lord. Its grain offering shall be two-tenths of an ephah of fine flour mixed with oil, an offering made by fire to the Lord, for a sweet aroma; and its drink offering shall be of wine, one-fourth of a hin. You shall eat neither bread nor parched grain nor fresh grain until the same day that you have brought an offering to your God; it shall be a statute forever throughout your generations in all your dwellings"''
(Leviticus 23:9-14).

We learn in verse 11 that the Feast of Firstfruits was to be celebrated on the day after the Sabbath. Jewish scholars have different opinions as to which Sabbath God intended, but it appears to have been the regular weekly Sabbath. This means that the Feast of Firstfruits was on the first day of the week, a Sunday.

The Hebrews were to bring the first sheaves *(omer)* of the barley harvest and wave them before the Lord. An *omer* was about four pints, or two quarts, or a half gallon of barley. Before any barley produce of the new crop could be eaten, or even touched, a measure had to be brought to the temple as an offering to the Lord. This offering is known as the *omer*.

The period of time between this feast and the Feast of Pentecost is a time of the "Counting of the *Omer*." The counting always started at day one and continued until day fifty, as follows: Today is the first day of the *omer*; today is the second day of the *omer*; today is the third day of the *omer*, etc.

By its very nature, physical work in the fields can cause us to forget our spiritual nature. Therefore, God gave the farmer these instructions so that he would remain conscious of his true purpose in life, which was to love, serve, and obey God, depending on Him for everything. By offering the firstfruits of his harvest to the Lord, the farmer was acknowledging his total dependence on God.

The Jewish people were to bring the first sheaves of the barley harvest and wave them before the Lord. A small plot of ground was set apart in the Kidron Valley to grow this firstfruits offering.

According to Alfred Edersheim in his book, *The Temple,* the sheaves were cut late in the afternoon, just before sunset. When the time for the cutting of the sheaf had arrived, a large, loud crowd of worshipers followed representative leaders to the place where the firstfruits were to be harvested. It was almost dark as they sang, played their instruments, danced, and celebrated the goodness of God. After the sheaf was cut, the people praised the Lord and retraced their path up the slopes of the Temple mount to the altar. It was now officially the "morrow after the Sabbath."[1]

Edersheim explains, "The ears were brought into the Court of the Temple, and thrashed out with canes or stalks, so as not to injure the corn; then parched on a pan perforated with holes, so that each grain might be touched by the fire. The omer was mixed with three-fourths of a pint of oil, and a handful of frankincense put on it, then waved before the Lord, and a handful taken out and burned on the altar."[2]

The purpose of this special service was to consecrate the harvest to God. The firstfruits represented the whole harvest. This act reminded the Hebrews that God had given them the land and that all of the harvest rightfully belonged to Him. The people were just stewards of the land. Offering the firstfruits actually consecrated the entire harvest to God. If God accepted the firstfruits of the harvest, it meant the entire harvest would be accepted by God.

HOW JESUS FULFILLED THE FEAST

Jesus fulfilled this feast when He was resurrected as the firstfruits from the dead. His resurrection marked the beginning of the harvest of souls who have been set apart for God through Jesus.

Paul spoke of Jesus as the fulfillment of this feast with these words, "But now Christ [Messiah] is risen from the dead, and has become the firstfruits of those who have fallen asleep. For since by man came death, by Man also came the resurrection of the dead. For in Adam all die, even so in Christ [Messiah] all shall be made alive. But each one in his own order: Christ [Messiah] the firstfruits, afterward those who are Christ's [Messiah's] at His coming" (1 Cor. 15:20-23).

Jesus was that human sheaf that God set apart for the purpose of conquering death and providing eternal life for all who would acknowledge Him as Messiah, Lord, and Savior. As such, He was the first who would rise from the dead never to die again.

Once again we refer to the chart titled *When was Jesus Crucified and Resurrected?* In fulfilling the Feast of Passover, Jesus was crucified on Wednesday, the 14th. To fulfill the Feast of Unleavened Bread, He was buried at the close of Wednesday and the beginning of Thursday, the 15th. He was resurrected at the close of the weekly Sabbath, the 17th and the beginning of the first day of the week, the Feast of First-fruits, the 18th.

Matthew gives the following account of Jesus' resurrection: "Now after the Sabbath [at the end or close of the Sabbath], as the first day of the week began to dawn [just as it began to get dark], Mary Magdalene and the other Mary came to see the tomb. And behold, there was a great earthquake; for an angel of the Lord descended from heaven, and came and rolled back the stone from the door, and sat on it. His countenance was like lightning, and his clothing as white as snow. And the guards shook for fear of him, and became like dead men. But the angel answered and said to the women, 'Do not be afraid, for I know that you seek Jesus, who was crucified. He is not here; for He is risen, as He said. Come, see the place where the Lord lay" (Matt. 28:1-6).

Let's read Matthew 28:1 again in light of its cultural context: "Now late on Sabbath, as it was getting dusk toward the first day of the week, Mary the Magdalene and the other Mary came to see the sepulcher." The proper understanding of this text indicates that the women came to the tomb late in the day or toward the end of the day. It does not mean after the day is over or completed. (See also John 20:1; Mark 16:9-11.)

John added some further details and mentioned the following statement Jesus made to Mary: "Do not cling to Me [touch Me not], for I have not yet ascended to My Father; but go to My brethren, and say to them, 'I am ascending to My Father and your Father, and to My God, and your God'" (John 20:17).

It was during this feast celebration at the temple that Jesus was resurrected. He was resurrected in the evening (sunset, not sunrise) at the time the firstfruits offering was cut and waved before God. As the barley sheaf could not be touched until it was offered to God, so Jesus, the human sheaf, could not be touched until He offered Himself in the heavenly temple as the firstfruits from the dead.

Jesus was going to ascend to the Father for the purpose of presenting Himself as the firstfruits from the dead. He is our great High Priest who offered Himself in fulfillment of the Feast of Firstfruits on the exact day the barley sheaves were being waved before the Lord.

The barley sheaf wave offering consisted of a number of individual barley stalks that had been bundled together. Likewise, when Jesus offered Himself as the firstfruits from the dead, many individual believers were raised with Him. Matthew explained:

> *"And the graves were opened; and many bodies of the saints who had fallen asleep were raised; and coming out of the graves after His resurrection, they went into the holy city and appeared to many"* (Matthew 27:52-53).

When the time came to harvest the crop, the farmer would go into his field and inspect the firstfruits of the crop. If he accepted the firstfruits, then the rest of the harvest would also be acceptable to him. Since our Heavenly Father has accepted Jesus as the firstfruits from the dead, believers are also acceptable to God through Jesus. He will also raise us from the dead and give us a new resurrected body fitted for eternity.

Paul expressed this truth to the Christians in Rome with these words:

> *"But if the Spirit of Him who raised Jesus from the dead dwells in you, He who raised Christ [Messiah] from the dead will also give life to your mortal bodies through His Spirit who dwells in you"* (Romans 8:11).

Jesus, as the firstfruits, is our representative. By presenting Himself, He consecrated the rest of us to the Father.

As Paul so clearly and boldly said to the Christians in Ephesus: "He [God] made us accepted in the Beloved" (Eph. 1:6). Believers are the human stalks that have been bundled together with Christ [Messiah]; therefore, "If the firstfruit is holy, the lump is also holy; and if the root is holy, so are the branches" (Rom. 11:16).

Paul writes to the Corinthian believers:

> *"Behold, I tell you a mystery; We shall not all sleep, but we shall all be changed—in a moment, in the twinkling of an eye, at the last trumpet. For the trumpet will sound, and the dead will be raised incorruptible, and we shall be changed. For this corruptible must put on incorruption, and this mortal must put on immortality. So when this corruptible has put on incorruption, and this mortal has put on immortality, then shall be brought to pass the saying that is written: 'Death is swallowed up in victory.' 'O Death, where is*

your sting? O Hades, where is your victory?' The sting of death is sin, and the strength of sin is the law. But thanks be to God, who gives us the victory through our Lord Jesus Christ [Yeshua the Messiah]. Therefore, my beloved brethren, be steadfast, immovable, always abounding in the work of the Lord, knowing that your labor is not in vain in the Lord" (1 Corinthians 15:51-58).

In his letter to the Thessalonian believers, Paul speaks further on this theme:

"But I do not want you to be ignorant, brethren, concerning those who have fallen asleep, lest you sorrow as others who have no hope. For if we believe that Jesus died and rose again, even so God will bring with Him those who sleep in Jesus. For this we say to you by the word of the Lord, that we who are alive and remain until the coming of the Lord will by no means precede those who are asleep. For the Lord Himself will descend from heaven with a shout, with the voice of an archangel, and with the trumpet of God. And the dead in Christ [Messiah] will rise first. Then we who are alive and remain shall be caught up together with them in the clouds to meet the Lord in the air. And thus we shall always be with the Lord" (1 Thessalonians 4:13-17).

In an additional word of comfort, Paul wrote:

"For God did not appoint us to wrath, but to obtain salvation through our Lord Jesus Christ [Messiah], who died for us, that whether we wake or sleep, we should live together with Him. Therefore, comfort each other and edify one another, just as you also are doing" (1 Thessalonians 5:9-11).

When Lazarus died, his sister came to Jesus for comfort. John recorded the following conversation:

> *"Now Martha, as soon as she heard that Jesus was coming, went and met Him, but Mary was sitting in the house. Now Martha said to Jesus, 'Lord, if You had been here, my brother would not have died. But even now I know that whatever you ask of God, God will give You.' Jesus said to her, 'Your brother will rise again.' Martha said to Him, 'I know that he will rise again in the resurrection at the last day.' Jesus said to her, 'I am the resurrection and the life. He who believes in Me, though he may die, he shall live. And whoever lives and believes in Me shall never die. Do you believe this?'"* (John 11:20-26).

Job expressed this hope for believers of all ages when he said, "For I know that my Redeemer lives, and He shall stand at last on the earth; and after my skin is destroyed, this I know, that in my flesh I shall see God" (Job 19:25-26).

Lord, may Your name be praised forever! May we know You at Passover, the fellowship of Your suffering at Unleavened Bread, and the power of Your resurrection at Firstfruits.

PERSONAL APPLICATION

The Feasts of Unleavened Bread and Firstfruits represent two important phases of Christian commitment that are necessary to change our spiritual condition. Unleavened Bread teaches about our burial with Jesus. This indicates we should live a life separated from the attitudes and ways of the world. This involves our putting off the old man of sin, characterized by the works of the flesh.

The Feast of Firstfruits teaches us about our resurrection with Jesus in our spirit as well as our future bodily resurrection. We are saved from our old life to live in the resurrected life of Messiah Jesus today. Putting off the old man is not enough. We must also put on the new man.

After Paul told the Ephesian believers to put off the old man, he then said, "And...put on the new man which was created according to God, in true righteousness and holiness" (Eph. 4:24). This new nature about which Paul is speaking is the very nature of God coming within us through the person of the Holy Spirit.

We put on this new man by allowing the Holy Spirit to live the resurrected life of Jesus through us. Paul had this exchange of natures in mind when he wrote, "Therefore, if anyone is in Christ [Messiah], he is a new creation; old things have passed away; behold, all things have become new" (2 Cor. 5:17). We who were dead in our trespasses and sins have been raised up with Jesus in our spirit-man to walk in newness of life.

Paul summarized this process in his letter to the Galatians:

> *"I have been crucified with Christ [Messiah]; it is no longer I who live, but Christ [Messiah] lives in me; and the life which I now live in the flesh I live by faith in the Son of God, who loved me and gave Himself for me"* (Galatians 2:20).

Paul underscored this understanding to the believers in Rome with these powerful words:

> *"Likewise you also, reckon yourselves to be dead indeed to sin, but alive to God in Christ [Messiah] Jesus our Lord. Therefore do not let sin reign in your mortal body, that you should obey it in its lusts. And do not present your members as instruments of unrighteousness to sin, but present yourselves to God as being alive from the dead, and your members as instruments of righteousness to God. For sin shall not have dominion*

over you, for you are not under law but under grace"
(Romans 6:11-14).

The new man Paul keeps speaking of is simply the Lord Himself living in us through the person of the Holy Spirit, as we learn from these words: "…Walk in the Spirit, and you shall not fulfill the lust of the flesh" (Gal. 5:16).

When we walk in the Spirit, the character of Messiah Jesus will be the dominant force in our life. Paul refers to the character of Jesus as the "fruit of the Spirit," which he describes with these words, "But the fruit of the Spirit is love, joy, peace, longsuffering, kindness, goodness, faithfulness, gentleness, self-control" (Gal. 5:22-23).

When we live in the character of Messiah Jesus, we not only have peace with God, but we also enjoy the peace of God (see Col. 3:15). Many believers do not experience this divine blessing because they have never separated themselves from the things of the world and consecrated themselves to Jesus as Lord of their life.

James wrote that we who have put our trust in Jesus and have received His Spirit are a kind of firstfruits of God's creatures (see James 1:18). He meant that we are the firstfruits of God's creation to experience the new life that God has decreed for the earth and its inhabitants through the redeeming work of Jesus. In view of this, we present ourselves as a living wave offering to God to show that we belong to Him.

PROPHETIC SEASONAL ASPECT

As mentioned in the previous chapter, the spiritual significance of both the Feasts of Unleavened Bread and Firstfruits were restored to the Church during the 1700s through the ministry of John and Charles Wesley.

John and Charles complemented each other in their ministry in a unique manner. Whereas John was a powerful preacher, Charles was a prolific songwriter. Recall from the last chapter that, in the course of their ministry, John traveled over 250,000 miles preaching the Gospel, mostly on horseback, while Charles penned over 6,000 Christian songs and poems. In this way, the people not only heard the Word of God, but they also learned to sing it. In many respects, Charles' songs had as much impact on the listeners as John's sermons.

Because their ministry was not received by the institutional Church (just as with Luther), the Wesleys were forced to take their message to the toiling masses of working-class people who had been ignored by the Church of England. Although they met considerable opposition, the grace and power of God worked through them mightily to breathe fresh life into the Church.

God used the Wesleys to radically change the society and social ills of their day. By emphasizing personal holiness and a change in one's condition as well as one's position, the Wesleys initiated a lasting spiritual renewal that restored Christian salt and light to a decaying and darkened world.[3]

PERSONAL STUDY REVIEW

1. Describe how Jesus fulfilled the Feast of Firstfruits.

2. How does the Feast of Firstfruits as revealed in Jesus apply to our lives today?

3. Describe the seasonal aspect of the Feast of Firstfruits.

4. Ask God to give you a personal encounter with Jesus as the spiritual reality of this feast.

ENDNOTES

1. Alfred Edersheim, *The Temple: Its Ministry and Services* (Peabody, MA: Hendrickson, 1994), 258-259.

2. Ibid.

3. For biographical information on the Wesleys, check these sites: http://wesley.nnu.edu/john-wesley; http://wesley.nnu.edu/charles-wesley.

CHAPTER 5

PENTECOST

The three feast seasons of Passover (Pesach), Pentecost (Shavuot), and Tabernacles (Succot) represent three major encounters God has with His covenant people. The feast season known as Passover was established by God for the purpose of teaching us how to find God's peace. We find peace with God when we appropriate Jesus as the Passover Lamb who died for our sins.

We find the peace of God through Jesus as our Unleavened Bread and Firstfruits representative. This work of Jesus benefits us personally when we set ourselves apart from the ways of the world and give ourselves completely to Jesus as our Lord and Master. This ongoing surrender produces godly character in our lives and gives us the peace of God.

While this is a great blessing we all need, it is certainly not all He has for us. God not only desires to give us His peace, but He also wants to give us His power. This is the purpose of the Feast of Pentecost. It represents the second major encounter we can have with God. Taken in order of the feasts, it is the fourth step we must take to walk in God's rest.

HISTORICAL BACKGROUND

God gives the following instructions concerning the Feast of Pentecost,

> "And you shall count for yourselves from the day after the Sabbath, from the day that you brought the sheaf of the wave offering: seven Sabbaths shall be completed. Count fifty days to the day after the seventh Sabbath; then you shall offer a new grain offering to the Lord. You shall bring from your dwellings two wave loaves of two-tenths of an ephah [3/5 of a bushel]. They shall be of fine flour; they shall be baked with leaven. They are the firstfruits to the Lord.

> "And you shall offer with the bread seven lambs of the first year, without blemish, one young bull, and two rams. They shall be as a burnt offering to the Lord, with their grain offering and their drink offerings, an offering made by fire for a sweet aroma to the Lord. Then you shall sacrifice one kid of the goats as a sin offering, and two male lambs of the first year as a sacrifice of a peace offering. The priests shall wave them with the bread of the firstfruits as a wave offering before the Lord, with the two lambs. They shall be holy to the Lord for the priests.

> "And you shall proclaim on the same day that it is a holy convocation to you. You shall do no customary work on it. It shall be a statute forever in all your dwellings throughout your generations" (Leviticus 23:15-21).

While the Feast of Passover marked the beginning of the barley harvest, the Feast of Pentecost was celebrated during the wheat harvest. Notice from the chart that it came on the sixth day of the

Hebrew month of Sivan. This corresponds to the Gentile months of May-June. The feast lasted for one day.

The instructions God gave us enable us to determine the exact day of the feast. God said they were to celebrate the feast fifty days after the Feast of Firstfruits. The Feast of Firstfruits was celebrated on the seventeenth of *Nisan*. Fifty days later falls on the sixth of *Sivan*. Since the word *Pentecost* in Greek means "fifty," this feast gets its name from the fifty-day interval between the two dates. The Feast of Pentecost was also referred to as the Feast of Weeks, Feast of Harvest, and the Day of Firstfruits (see Exod. 23:16; Num. 28:26).

The main activity on the Feast of Pentecost was the presentation of a wave offering to the Lord. This was two loaves of bread baked with leaven. This bread was made of fine flour that had been carefully sifted to separate the coarse matter from the wheat. The wave offering expressed the Hebrews' dependence on God for the harvest and their daily bread. It was a thanksgiving offering.

Later when the Jews were scattered among the nations, the Feast of Pentecost lost its primary significance as a harvest festival and was celebrated as a memorial to the time when God gave them the Torah at Mount Sinai.

Jewish sages have traditionally taught that God gave the Torah to Moses on the day of Pentecost.[1] We learn in Exodus 19 that the Jews arrived at Mount Sinai in the third month on the Hebrew calendar and possibly on the third day.

Exodus 19:1 reads, "In the third month after the children of Israel had gone out of the land of Egypt, on the same day, they came to the Wilderness of Sinai." The phrase "same day" is interpreted to refer to the phrase "third month." The understanding is that they came to Sinai on the third day of the third month. Three days later, on the sixth of *Sivan*, God came down upon Mount Sinai and gave them the Torah (verse 11).

The following verses tell us what happened:

"Then it came to pass on the third day, in the morning, that there were thunderings and lightnings, and a thick cloud on the mountain; and the sound of the trumpet was very loud, so that all the people who were in the camp trembled. And Moses brought the people out of the camp to meet with God, and they stood at the foot of the mountain.

"Now Mount Sinai was completely in smoke, because the Lord descended upon it in fire. Its smoke ascended like the smoke of a furnace, and the whole mountain quaked greatly. And when the blast of the trumpet sounded long and became louder and louder, Moses spoke, and God answered him by voice. Then the Lord came down upon Mount Sinai, on the top of the mountain. And the Lord called Moses to the top of the mountain, and Moses went up" (Exodus 19:16-20).

The English translation says all the people witnessed the thunderings and the lightnings. Jewish scholars believe that the people actually "saw the voice of God" coming out of the mountain in tongues of fire. The mixed multitude that came out of Egypt saw the tongues of fire and heard the one voice of God speak in their different languages so they could understand His words. Since it seems strange to "see voices," this phrase was translated as thunderings and lightnings. The voices sounded like thundering and appeared as fire.[2]

Psalm 29 is about the awesome power of the voice of the Lord. In one of the statements referring to the Exodus experience, we read, "The voice of the Lord divides the flames of fire" (Ps. 29:7).

The writer of the Book of Hebrews also refers to this event and uses similar statements:

"For you have not come to the mountain that may be touched and that burned with fire, and to blackness and darkness and tempest, and the sound of a trumpet and the voice of words, so that those who heard it begged that the word should not be spoken to them anymore" (Hebrews 12:18-19).

After God gave the first of His holy words (commandments), we read:

"Now all the people witnessed the thunderings, the lightning flashes, the sound of the trumpet, and the mountain smoking; and when the people saw it, they trembled and stood afar off. Then they said to Moses, 'You speak with us, and we will hear; but let not God speak with us, lest we die.' And Moses said to the people, 'Do not fear; for God has come to test you, and that His fear may be before you, so that you may not sin'" (Exodus 20:18-20).

So God came down upon Mount Sinai to meet with His people. They gathered in one place in the morning on the sixth of Sivan. The whole mountain was filled with fire. The trumpet sounded loudly. The people ran to the foot of the mountain to meet with God. They saw voices in fire. God spoke, and then Moses spoke. The people trembled. It was an awesome revelation of the glory of God. Yet, because of their sin, three thousand were to die (see Exod. 32:28).

What we learn from Scripture and the ancient interpretation from Jewish scholars is that the first Pentecost did not happen in the Book of Acts. It happened in the book of Exodus.[3] If you know your Bible, you are probably already making this connection. The first Pentecost was at Mount Sinai when God wrote His words on tablets of stone. Yet, the Lord promised there would be a time in the distant future when He would write His laws on the fleshly tablets of their hearts. (See Jeremiah 31:31-34.)

The people would come to Jerusalem each year celebrating Pentecost hoping that God would fulfill His word to write His laws on their hearts. For 1,500 years they went home disappointed. But God is faithful to keep His word. In His own appointed time, God would come down on the people. Not on Mount Sinai in the desert, but on Mount Zion in Jerusalem. Hallelujah!

HOW JESUS FULFILLED THE FEAST

Jesus fulfilled the Feast of Pentecost when He was glorified and exalted to the throne of God; He then sent the Holy Spirit upon His disciples on the Day of Pentecost. This was the fulfillment (spiritual reality) of what God had promised through the prophets. God would write His laws on their hearts through the giving of the Holy Spirit. Remember, this was a Feast of the Lord the Jews had been celebrating for centuries. It was not a new revelation. They had been waiting for centuries.

Jesus spoke of Himself as the fulfillment of this feast with the following words:

> *"...The hour has come that the Son of Man should be glorified. Most assuredly, I say to you, unless a grain of wheat falls into the ground and dies, it remains alone; but if it dies, it produces much grain"* (John 12:23-24).

Jesus was talking about Himself as the human grain of wheat who would die for the sins of the world. The bread was made with fine flour, which represents perfect righteousness. Jesus was perfectly righteous. There was no coarse matter (sin) in Him. Yet, as the wheat was crushed, sifted, and baked in order to become bread, so Jesus was crushed, sifted, and baked for our sins. However, because He had never sinned, death could not hold Jesus (see Rev. 1:18). Because of His perfect life, Jesus was resurrected as the firstfruits from the dead.

As we've just learned, it was fifty days from the Feast of Firstfruits to the Feast of Pentecost. Likewise, it was exactly fifty days from Jesus' resurrection to the day when He sent the Holy Spirit upon His disciples (refer to the chart).

The Day of Pentecost did not originate with Christianity. It is the feast day upon which God chose to send the Holy Spirit as proof that Jesus had been exalted as Lord. This was the day when the Jews would be in Jerusalem celebrating the feast and the giving of the Torah.

On the evening that Jesus was resurrected, He appeared to His disciples and breathed eternal life into them. John recorded this event:

> *"Then, the same day at evening, being the first day of the week, when the doors were shut where the disciples were assembled, for fear of the Jews, Jesus came and stood in the midst, and said to them, 'Peace be with you.' When He had said this, He showed them His hands and His side. Then the disciples were glad when they saw the Lord. So Jesus said to them again, 'Peace to you! As the Father has sent Me, I also send you.' And when He had said this, He breathed on them, and said to them, 'Receive the Holy Spirit'"* (John 20:19-22).

At this moment, the disciples experienced a spiritual rebirth that established their new life position in Jesus. But Jesus had more for them. He desired to fill them with the Holy Spirit so they would have power to be His witnesses to the nations. However, it was not yet time for Him to do this.

Therefore, Jesus spent the next forty days with the disciples explaining how the Hebrew Scriptures pointed to Himself as their fulfillment. Then when the time came for Jesus to ascend back to Heaven, He told the disciples to wait in Jerusalem until He would send the Promise of the Father, at which time they would be filled with the Holy Spirit.

Luke tells us the story:

> *"Then He said to them, 'These are the words which I spoke to you while I was still with you, that all things must be fulfilled which were written in the Law of Moses and the Prophets and the Psalms concerning Me.' And He opened their understanding, that they might comprehend the Scriptures. Then He said to them, 'Thus it is written, and thus it was necessary for the Christ [Messiah] to suffer and rise from the dead the third day, and that repentance and remission of sins should be preached in His name to all nations, beginning at Jerusalem. And you are witnesses of these things. Behold, I send the Promise of My Father upon you; but tarry in the city of Jerusalem until you are endued with power from on high.'*
>
> *"And He led them out as far as Bethany, and He lifted up His hands and blessed them. Now it came to pass, while He blessed them, that He was parted from them and carried up into heaven. And they worshipped Him, and returned to Jerusalem with great joy, and were continually in the temple praising and blessing God. Amen"* (Luke 24:44-53).

Later in the Book of Acts, Luke recalls the conversation Jesus had with His disciples. He wrote:

> *"And being assembled together with them, He commanded them not to depart from Jerusalem, but to wait for the Promise of the Father, 'which,' He said,*

'you have heard from Me; for John truly baptized with water, but you shall be baptized with the Holy Spirit not many days from now.' Therefore, when they had come together, they asked Him, saying, 'Lord will you at this time restore the kingdom to Israel?' And He said to them, 'It is not for you to know times or seasons which the Father has put in His own authority. But you shall receive power when the Holy Spirit has come upon you; and you shall be witnesses to Me in Jerusalem, and in all Judea and Samaria, and to the end of the earth'" (Acts 1:4-8).

Luke reviews the words of Jesus instructing His disciples to wait in Jerusalem until they receive the Promise of the Father, which Jesus calls the baptism in the Holy Spirit. Jesus says the purpose of this baptism in the Holy Spirit is to give the disciples power to be witnesses to Jesus. They would have this encounter with the Holy Spirit ten days later on the Day of Pentecost.

About 120 of Jesus' followers then gathered in an upper room waiting in prayer for this blessed event. Luke records what happened on that glorious day:

"When the Day of Pentecost had fully come, they were all with one accord in one place. And suddenly there came a sound from heaven, as of a rushing mighty wind, and it filled the whole house where they were sitting. Then there appeared to them divided tongues as of fire, and one sat upon each of them. And they were all filled with the Holy Spirit and began to speak with other tongues, as the Spirit gave them utterance.

"And there were dwelling in Jerusalem Jews, devout men, from every nation under heaven. And when this sound occurred, the multitude came together, and were confused, because everyone heard them speak in

his own language. Then they were all amazed and marveled, saying to one another, 'Look, are not all these who speak Galileans? And how is it that we hear, each in our own language in which we were born?'" (Acts 2:1-8).

From Luke's account, we see the marvelous timing of God. Thousands of Jews had come to Jerusalem to celebrate the Feast of Pentecost. This feast symbolized their second major encounter with God. But it was only a foreshadowing of what was to come.

While it is true that God gave them the Torah on this very day, the Torah could not provide them with power. It was not the Promise of the Father. The reality that the Feast of Pentecost had illustrated for centuries was the anointing of the disciples with spiritual power for the purpose of enabling them to be effective witnesses of Jesus as Messiah, Savior, and Lord.

According to Luke's record, when the disciples were filled with the Holy Spirit, they began to worship God in the foreign languages that were spoken and understood by the Jewish pilgrims who had come to Jerusalem to keep the feast. These were languages that the disciples themselves did not know. There was such a loud noise accompanying this experience that it attracted the attention of the Jewish pilgrims, who went to see what the commotion was all about.

Instead of rushing to the foot of Mount Sinai, the crowds rushed to the foot of Mount Zion. As they approached, they heard the disciples worshiping God in the various languages represented by the Jews' homeland. As their ancestors had experienced at Mount Sinai, the people saw and heard tongues of fire. The crowds thought the disciples were drunk. But Peter noted that it was only nine o'clock in the morning, much too early to be drunk (see Acts 2:15).

Peter then stood up and preached a bold sermon to this Jewish crowd. When they heard his words, the people trembled and sought salvation. Instead of three thousand dying, as happened at Mount

Sinai, three thousand accepted Jesus as Messiah and Lord (see Acts 2:37-42). This outpouring of the Holy Spirit was taking place on the very day that the Jews were offering the two wave loaves to God symbolizing their dependence on Him.

Remember that the two waves were baked with leaven (a common symbol of sin). One of these wave loaves was pointing to the Jews, who, although they were sinners, received the power of God in their lives by acknowledging Jesus as Messiah and Lord (the fine flour). This happened on the exact day the Jews had been celebrating the Feast of Pentecost for almost 1,500 years.

But what about the other loaf? The other loaf represented the Gentiles, who would also receive this wonderful blessing from God, even though they too were sinners. When Peter preached his sermon to the Jews, he said that the Promise of the Father (baptism in the Holy Spirit) was for everyone who would acknowledge Jesus as Lord (see Acts 2:39).

The dramatic outpouring of the Holy Spirit on the Gentiles was to take place in the coastal town of Caesarea. There was a Gentile by the name of Cornelius who was seeking God with all his heart. An angel spoke to him in a vision instructing him to send for Peter, who would come and preach to him and his friends.

Luke tells us the story in Acts 10:44-47:

> *"While Peter was still speaking these words, the Holy Spirit fell upon all those who heard the word. And those of the circumcision who believed were astonished, as many as came with Peter, because the gift of the Holy Spirit had been poured out on the Gentiles also. For they heard them speak with tongues and magnify God. Then Peter answered, 'Can any forbid water, that these should not be baptized who have received the Holy Spirit just as we have?'"*

Later, when Peter shared what happened at that meeting with his fellow Jewish believers, he said:

"And as I began to speak, the Holy Spirit fell upon them, as upon us at the beginning. Then I remembered the word of the Lord, how He said, 'John indeed baptized with water, but you shall be baptized with the Holy Spirit'" (Acts 11:15-16).

Now we can see the significance of the fine flour and the two wave loaves of leaven. The fine flour represented Jesus, who was perfectly righteous and without sin. The two wave loaves represented the Jew and the Gentile. Both have the leaven of sin in their lives. But both can receive the power of God to help them overcome sin and live as effective witnesses to the lordship of Jesus.

PERSONAL APPLICATION

John the Baptist introduced Jesus as the Lamb of God who takes away the sin of the world and baptizes in the Holy Spirit (see John 1:29; Matt. 3:11; Mark 1:8; Luke 3:16). Jesus fulfilled the Feast of Passover as the Lamb of God who died for our sins. He fulfilled the Feast of Pentecost as the exalted and glorified Lord who baptizes in the Holy Spirit.

Passover represents the first major encounter with God by His covenant people. Pentecost represents the second encounter. God wants us to know Jesus, not only as the Lamb of God who died for our sins, but also as the living, glorified Messiah and Lord who baptizes us in the Holy Spirit.

If there was ever a group of people who should have been prepared to minister in the power of the Holy Spirit, it was the disciples. They had Jesus as their teacher for over three years. They watched Him perform many miracles. They saw Him conquer death and stand in their midst in a resurrected body. Jesus gave them the indwelling Holy Spirit, and they were born again to eternal life.

Yet, in spite of all of this, Jesus told them to wait in Jerusalem until they received His power. The purpose of the baptism in the Holy Spirit was to give the disciples, and us, power to be bold witnesses to the lordship of Jesus (see Acts 1:8). It was this second major encounter with God, rather than the resurrection, that transformed Peter from being a coward hiding behind closed doors to the man who stood before the great crowd and boldly proclaimed Jesus to be Messiah and Lord.

Peter had become a different man. He was no longer timid. Neither were the other disciples who were there with him. After they were filled with the Holy Spirit, they began to minister in the power, boldness, and authority of Jesus Himself. This little group of ordinary men and women turned their world upside down. When they were born again at Passover, they received the indwelling Spirit for salvation. At Pentecost, they were empowered and filled to overflowing with the Holy Spirit for service. It was another encounter with God beyond their basic salvation experience.

Even Jesus had to be filled with the Holy Spirit before beginning His ministry. He had to have God's power working in His life before He preached, healed the sick, cast out demons, and overcame satan.

Jesus was filled with the Holy Spirit when He was baptized by John in the Jordan River. Matthew gives the following account: "When He had been baptized, Jesus came up immediately from the water; and behold, the heavens were open to Him, and He saw the Spirit of God descending like a dove and alighting upon Him. And suddenly a voice came from heaven, saying, 'This is My beloved Son, in whom I am well pleased'" (Matt. 3:16-17).

Now that Jesus was filled with the Holy Spirit, He was ready to begin His ministry. After a brief victorious encounter with satan,

Jesus went to Galilee. The Bible says He went in the power of the Holy Spirit (see Luke 4:14).

While in Galilee, Jesus visited His hometown of Nazareth. He went to the synagogue and stood up to read the Scriptures. The leader of the synagogue gave Jesus the Book of Isaiah, from which He began to read these words: "The Spirit of the Lord is upon Me, because He has anointed Me to preach the gospel to the poor. He has sent Me to heal the brokenhearted, to proclaim liberty to the captives and recovery of sight to the blind, to set at liberty those who are oppressed, to proclaim the acceptable year of the Lord" (Luke 4:18-19).

This is the ministry of Jesus. It is also the great commission Jesus has given to all His followers. He told His disciples, "...he who believes in Me, the works that I do he will do also; and greater works than these he will do, because I go to My Father" (John 14:12).

Jesus said His followers would do greater works than He did because He was going to His Father. When Jesus went to His heavenly Father, He sent the Holy Spirit upon the disciples. When the Holy Spirit came upon the disciples, they received power to minister in the Spirit. They were the beginning of Jesus' promise that we would do greater works than He did.

When Jesus walked the earth, His ministry was limited to His human body. But now He ministers on earth through His spiritual body, the body of Messiah called the Church. However, just as Jesus and the first disciples needed the empowering of the Holy Spirit, His followers today must be filled with the Holy Spirit. God still wants to use ordinary men and women to turn the world upside down as we minister in the boldness and power of the Holy Spirit.

PROPHETIC SEASONAL ASPECT

As the Book of Acts reveals, the New Covenant people of God began in a blaze of glory. God worked mightily through the early believers. Jesus gave them the following commission and assurance: "And He said to them, 'Go into all the world and preach the gospel to every creature. He who believes and is baptized will be saved; but he who does not believe will be condemned. And these signs will follow those who believe: In My name they will cast out demons; they will speak with new tongues; they will take up serpents; and if they drink anything deadly, it will by no means hurt them; they will lay hands on the sick, and they will recover'" (Mark 16:15-18).

Mark further wrote, "So then, after the Lord had spoken to them, He was received up into heaven, and sat down at the right hand of God. And they went out and preached everywhere, the Lord working with them and confirming the word through the accompanying signs. Amen" (Mark 16:19-20).

When the Church became institutionalized in A.D. 312, many of those in charge were politicians rather than godly, spiritual men. The result was that Christianity was organized into a religious system whose leaders chose a human-directed structure rather than a Spirit-led and empowered Church. The spiritual reality of the Feast of Pentecost was lost to the Church for centuries. Yet, throughout Church history, there have been periodic, localized revivals of Pentecost. God began to restore Pentecost on a worldwide basis in the early 1900s. There were two significant events.

The first event took place on New Year's Day, 1901, at Bethel Bible College in Topeka, Kansas. Charles Parham was teaching on the baptism in the Holy Spirit and encouraging his students to search the Scriptures regarding the subject. It was during this time of study that a Miss Agnes Ozman received the gift of speaking in tongues. Parham and several students had a similar experience three days later.

This Pentecostal message, with its accompanying manifestations, soon spread to the surrounding states and made its way into Texas and finally out to California in 1906.

A man named William Seymour arrived in Los Angeles to preach at a Nazarene Church but was not received because of his Pentecostal message. He then began to hold services in a converted livery stable at 312 Azusa Street. It was at this location that a mighty Pentecostal revival started that lasted for three years. This revival launched the modern worldwide Pentecostal movement. As news of the revival spread, many Christians from around the world came to the meetings at Azusa Street and took the message of Pentecost back with them to their homeland.

Because man is reluctant to hand over the leadership of the Church to the Holy Spirit, this restoration of the Feast of Pentecost was rejected by the leaders of the mainline Christian denominations (just as with Luther and Wesley).

In the late 1950s and early 1960s, God again moved to restore the Feast of Pentecost to the Church in what became known as the "charismatic renewal." This more recent revival of Pentecost has influenced all the historic Christian denominations, both Protestant and Catholic. While still rejected by much of the institutional Church, it may be argued that most Christians today are Pentecostal, non-white, and from emerging, third-world countries.[4]

PERSONAL STUDY REVIEW

1. Describe how Jesus fulfilled the Feast of Pentecost.

2. How does the Feast of Pentecost as revealed in Jesus apply to our lives today?

3. Describe the seasonal aspect of the Feast of Pentecost.

4. Ask God to give you a personal encounter with Jesus as the spiritual reality of this feast.

ENDNOTES

1. See http://ffoz.org/resources/articles/appointed_times/ shavuot.php.

2. Ibid.

3. Ibid.

4. See www.geocities.com/ccom_ctbi/ccom_AGM_files/ 020913-15_CCOM_AGM_Allan_Anderson.htm.

CHAPTER 6

TRUMPETS

The Feast of Tabernacles was the last of the required feast seasons. It included the Feasts of Trumpets, Atonement, and Tabernacles. As with Passover and Pentecost, all the Jewish males were required to journey to Jerusalem for its celebration.

The Feast of Tabernacles was celebrated during the Hebrew month of *Tishri*. This was at the end of the harvest season. It is also called the Feast of Ingathering (see Exod. 23:16). By this time, all the harvest was complete, and both the land and people were at rest.

The clear teaching of this feast season was that God wanted His covenant people to learn to rest in Him. Therefore, the Feast of Tabernacles represents the third major encounter the believer can have with God through the person and work of Messiah Jesus.

While the Feast of Passover teaches us about God's peace and the Feast of Pentecost teaches us about God's power, the Feast of Tabernacles teaches us about God's rest. God's rest is the place believers come to in their walk with God where they find contentment in God just for who He is in His nature and being.

Before learning about this feast, it would be helpful for us to consider the period on the Hebrew calendar when there was no feast. These were the long summer months of *Tammuz*, *Ab*, and *Elul*.

As we've learned, the feasts were religious seasons or holy convocations representing God's dealings with the Jewish people as a nation. They symbolized major encounters between God and His covenant people. The long, hot summer months when there was no feast served as a prophetic picture to the Jewish people of a future period of time when God would not be dealing with them on a national basis. He would still be redeeming individual Jews, but His attention would be directed toward the Gentiles.

God chose the Jews as the nation of people through whom He would work out certain of His divine plans and purposes. God would use them to write down and preserve the Scriptures, to bring Messiah into the world, and to proclaim the Gospel of Jesus to all nations. The Jews fulfilled these first two callings but failed on the last because their leaders rejected Jesus as the Messiah.

When the Jews as a nation rejected Jesus, God directed His attention primarily toward the Gentiles. John said of Jesus, "He came to His own [Jews], and His own did not receive Him. But as many as received Him, to them [Gentiles] He gave the right to become children of God, to those who believe in His name" (John 1:11-12).

For the last 2,000 years God has blessed the Gentiles, not Israel. While God's covenant with the Jewish people is unconditional and forever in time, the Gentiles have been the ones to spread the Gospel of Jesus to the world. This span of time in history when God's attention is directed toward the Gentiles will continue up to the future prophetic fulfillment of the Feast of Tabernacles. Therefore, the three long summer months where there is no feast corresponds to what some call "the Church period." Please note this on the Feasts chart. It is really the time of God calling the Gentiles into His Kingdom.

I use the phrase "Church period" simply because that is the commonly understood term for this period in God's redemptive history.

But because there is still another feast that will be literally fulfilled in the future, we understand that there will come a time when God will turn His attention back to the Jews and once again deal with them on a national basis. This third and final encounter is the return of Messiah Jesus in power and glory to establish the Kingdom of God on the earth. This is the prophetic significance of the Feast of Tabernacles.

Now that Israel has been restored as a nation, and the Jews once again control Jerusalem, we can be assured that God is even now dealing with the Jewish people as a nation to prepare them for the coming of Messiah Jesus. This is what is happening in our world today. As we see Israel in the spotlight of world news, we can know that the return of Messiah Jesus is near even if the nations force Israel to divide Jerusalem.

God amazingly revealed that this was His plan by strategically placing a comment about Gentiles in Leviticus 23. God put this comment right between the last verse of instruction on the Feast of Pentecost and the first verse of instruction of the Feast of Trumpets, which is part of the Feast of Tabernacles. Perhaps God did this as a sneak preview of what He had in mind all along. Here is the comment, "When you reap the harvest of your land, you shall not wholly reap the corners of your field when you reap, nor shall you gather any gleaning from your harvest. You shall leave them for the poor and for the stranger: I am the Lord your God" (Lev. 23:22).

The key word for the purposes of this discussion is *stranger*. It refers to Gentiles. The story of Ruth and Boaz was written in the Bible as an example of this particular instruction from God being obeyed.

Boaz was a rich Jewish landowner. Ruth was a Gentile (Moabite) who gleaned in his fields. Ruth married Boaz and as a result, became a partaker in the covenant promises God had made to Father Abraham (see Gen. 17). Likewise, the Gentiles have become partakers in certain of the covenant promises to Abraham through their spiritual marriage to Jesus. (Boaz is a type or shadow of Jesus, while Ruth is a type of the Gentile Church.)

The Gentile Church period fills the great time gap between the two comings of Jesus. He came the first time as the Passover Lamb who died for our sins. Then He sent the Holy Spirit to initiate the age of the Gentile Church. When the Gentile Church age is over, He will come a second time as the Lion from the tribe of Judah to rule, not only as King of the Jews, but also as King of kings and Lord of lords.

The prophetic significance of the Feast of Tabernacles is that it represents the end of the age and the return of Messiah Jesus in God's final encounter with the Jewish people. Paul summarizes all of this in Romans 9 through 11. As fascinating as this subject is, we must leave it now to learn about the Feast of Trumpets.

HISTORICAL BACKGROUND

God gave the following instructions concerning the Feast of Trumpets: "Then the Lord spoke to Moses, saying, 'Speak to the children of Israel saying: "In the seventh month, on the first day of the month, you shall have a sabbath-rest, a memorial of blowing of trumpets, a holy convocation. You shall do no customary work on it; and you shall offer an offering made by fire to the Lord"'" (Lev. 23:23-25).

We learn from this Scripture reference that the Feast of Trumpets was on the first day of the seventh month on the religious calendar (see the chart). This is the Hebrew month of *Tishri,* which corresponds to the months of September-October on the Gentile calendar. *Tishri* is also the first month on the Jewish civil calendar and is the Jewish New Year. The Hebrew name for this beginning of the year is *Rosh HaShanah,* which means "Head of the Year."

The main purpose of the Feast of Trumpets was to announce the arrival of the seventh month in order to prepare the people for the Day of Atonement, which was ten days later. The seventh month was special because it was the last month in the religious season. It was the time when God would complete His dealings with the people for that year. It was also the last time they were required to journey to Jerusalem until the following year at Passover.

The day was not marked by any special events other than the blowing of trumpets and the offering of sacrifices (see Num. 29:1-6). The Hebrews always blew trumpets on the first day of each month so everyone would know the new month had arrived (see Num. 10:10). But on the Feast of Trumpets, they blew them extra long and extra loud throughout the day.

The type of trumpet blown was the ram's horn, for which the Hebrew word is *shofar.* The *shofar* was blown in remembrance of the ram that was sacrificed in place of Isaac (see Gen. 22:13). Jewish tradition teaches that God blew one of the ram's horns at Mount Sinai at Pentecost and will blow the other ram's horn at the coming of Messiah.

God used trumpets in the Hebrew Bible as a means of communicating with His covenant people. God could not speak directly to the people without terrifying them. So He spoke to them indirectly through the use of trumpets. To the Hebrews, the sound of the trumpet represented both the voice of God and the might of God in warfare. A good summary of how the trumpets were used is provided in the tenth chapter of the Book of Numbers.

Originally, two silver trumpets were blown, but they were later replaced by the *shofar.* The silver trumpets were made from the same source of silver. They were blown to assemble the people to worship, to break camp, and as an alarm in preparation for battle.[1]

One of the clearest demonstrations of the use of trumpets in warfare is the story of Joshua at the battle of Jericho. Moses had died, and the leadership passed to Joshua, who became responsible for leading the people into the Promised Land.

Joshua encountered one who identified himself as the commander of the army of the Lord (see Josh. 5:13-15). This commander of God's army gave Joshua a strange battle plan. It is one that Joshua would have never thought of himself. And if he had, he certainly wouldn't have told anyone. They would have thought he was crazy. But God doesn't do things the way man does.

Are you ready for this? The angel told Joshua to march his army around the city of Jericho once each day for six days. Seven priests were to follow the army, each blowing a *shofar*. They were followed by another group of priests carrying the Ark of the Covenant. They were followed by a rear guard. All were to march in absolute silence. No one was to say a word. The only noise was the sound of the *shofars* blown by the priests.

On the seventh day, they were to march around the city seven times. Everyone was to be quiet. Then at a certain point, Joshua was to give a command for the priests to blow one long, loud blast on the *shofar*. Then everyone was to shout! At that very moment, according to the commander of God's army, the walls of Jericho would fall down, enabling the Hebrews to take the city. (See Joshua 6.)

Joshua carried out the battle plan given to him by the commander of God's army. It all happened just as God said, and the Jews soundly defeated their enemy.

As God spoke to the people and used trumpets to fight their battles for them, the Jews began to call God the "horn of their salvation." By this, they meant that God was their deliverer who would fight their battles for them and save them from their enemies.

King David was a great warrior who clearly understood and appreciated the might of God in warfare. He spoke of God as the horn of his salvation. In Psalm 18, David says to God, "I will love you, O Lord, my strength. The Lord is my rock and my fortress and my deliverer; my God, my strength, in whom I will trust; my shield and the horn of my salvation; my stronghold. I will call upon the Lord who is worthy to be praised; so shall I be saved from my enemies" (Ps. 18:1-3). (See also Second Samuel 22:3.)

How Jesus Fulfilled the Feast

From a Christian perspective, Jesus is the true Commander of the army of God (see Rev. 19:11-16). When Zacharias learned that the Messiah was to be born, he declared these words concerning Him: "Blessed is the Lord God of Israel, for He has visited and redeemed His people, and has raised up a horn of salvation for us in the house of His servant David, as He spoke by the mouth of His holy prophets, who have been since the world began, that we should be saved from our enemies and from the hand of all who hate us" (Luke 1:68-71).

Zacharias referred to Messiah Jesus as the horn of salvation who would save them from their enemies. In the first century, the enemy the Jews wanted to be saved from was Rome. The Jews were looking for a great deliverer who would overthrow the Roman Empire and establish the kingdom of David. Yet, in His first coming, Jesus' purpose was not to destroy the Roman Empire. His purpose was to destroy the works of satan and the sin in men's hearts that made possible the evil and oppression of Rome.

As the Commander of the army of God and the horn of our salvation, Jesus defeated the enemies of our soul. But His victory was not an easy one. His adversary satan did not give up without a fight. There was a great spiritual battle. Immediately after Jesus was filled with the Holy Spirit, He encountered spiritual warfare. As Jesus drew near to God in preparation for His ministry, satan came to tempt Him. Yet Jesus overcame satan's temptations (see Matt. 4:1-11).

Paul says that Jesus disarmed or spoiled principalities and powers (satan and his demons) and triumphed over them (see Col. 2:15). The word *spoiled* means to carry away as a captive. It refers to an ancient military practice. When a general conquered his enemy, a great homecoming parade would be given in his honor. This was called the "parade of triumph." When the general came into the city, he would strip the opposing king, whom he had taken captive, of all his armor. Then he would march him down the main street of the parade. The whole city would turn out for the parade to cheer the general and celebrate the victory. They then gave the victorious general the keys to the city.[2]

Do you see the parallel? By His death and resurrection, Jesus disarmed satan and took him captive. When Jesus returned to Heaven, God the Father prepared a big homecoming parade for Him. It was the great parade of triumph. All the angels of Heaven came out to meet Jesus. They lined the streets of Heaven and sang, "...worthy is the Lamb who was slain to receive power and riches and wisdom, and strength and honor and glory and blessing!" (Rev. 5:12). Then God the Father gave Jesus the keys to death and Hades (see Rev. 1:18).

Paul wrote to the Ephesians that God the Father has given Jesus a position "far above all principality and power and might and dominion, and every name that is named, not only in this age, but also in that which is to come. And He put all things under His feet..." (Eph. 1:21-22).

Paul also wrote of Jesus' exaltation to the Philippian believers, "Therefore God also has highly exalted Him and given Him the name which is above every name, that at the name of Jesus every knee should bow, of those in heaven, and of those on earth, and of those under the earth, and that every tongue should confess that Jesus Christ [Yeshua the Messiah] is Lord, to the glory of God the Father" (Phil. 2:9-11).

Peter writes of Jesus, "who has gone into heaven and is at the right hand of God, angels and authorities and powers having been made subject to Him" (1 Pet. 3:22).

Jesus spoke of a physical kingdom as well as a spiritual kingdom. But the physical kingdom could only be established by accepting the spiritual kingdom. Although tens of thousands of Jews acknowledged Jesus as Messiah, the leadership in Jerusalem rejected Him. Jesus then offered the spiritual blessing of the Kingdom of God to Gentiles as well as believing Jews. While the physical kingdom will be realized at the coming of Messiah Jesus, believers presently live in the spiritual realm of the Kingdom of God.

When God completes His time of calling the Gentiles to Himself, He will once again turn His attention to the Jewish people on a national basis. The Jewish people as a nation will acknowledge Jesus as Messiah and King (see Zech. 12:10; Rom. 11:25-26). Jesus will then return to earth to defeat the enemy nations who will be seeking to destroy the Jews (see Zech. 14:1-9). At that time, God Himself will rule as King over all the earth through Messiah Jesus. Both the Kingdom of God and the kingdom of David will be united in His rule (see Isa. 9:6-7). Now that we see Israel reborn as a nation, we can know that the coming of Messiah is near.

PERSONAL APPLICATION

You've probably already figured out that the Feast of Trumpets relates to the believer's spiritual warfare. Once we experience the reality of the Feast of Pentecost and are filled with the Holy Spirit, we will experience spiritual warfare. The closer we draw to God, the more our spiritual battles intensify. We become a threat to satan. He will do anything to defeat us. Learning to live in the victory of Jesus as the "Horn of our Salvation" is a prerequisite to entering the rest of God. Thus, the Feast of Trumpets symbolizes the fifth step in our walk with God.

Paul identifies our real enemy with these words, "Finally, my brethren, be strong in the Lord and in the power of His might. Put on the whole armor of God, that you may be able to stand against the wiles of the devil. For we do not wrestle against flesh and blood, but against principalities, against powers, against the rulers of the darkness of this age, against spiritual hosts of wickedness in the heavenly places" (Eph. 6:10-12).

We learn from Paul's words that our real enemy is the devil and a great host of demon followers that make up his army. Jesus has defeated the devil! Our strength and power come from God through Jesus as the trumpet of God. Paul expressed it this way to the believers in Corinth, "For though we walk in the flesh, we do not war according to the flesh. For the weapons of our warfare are not carnal but mighty through God for pulling down strongholds" (2 Cor. 10:3-4).

God has defeated satan for us through Messiah Jesus. This means we don't have to try to defeat him ourselves. He is already defeated. We simply stand in the victory God has already won for us. We do this by putting on the spiritual armor of God.

Paul describes this armor for us in these words: "Therefore take up the whole armor of God, that you may be able to withstand in the evil day, and having done all, to stand. Stand therefore, having girded your waist with truth, having put on the breastplate of righteousness, and having shod your feet with the preparation of the gospel of peace; above all, taking the shield of faith with which you will be able to quench all the fiery darts of the wicked one. And take the helmet of salvation, and the sword of the Spirit, which is the word of God; praying always with all prayer and supplication in the Spirit, being watchful to this end with all perseverance and supplication for all the saints" (Eph. 6:13-18).

Paul mentions six pieces of armor. Each piece represents an aspect of the Lord Himself as the trumpet of God. Taken as a whole, they provide a symbolic description of the person and work of Jesus in defeating satan for us. Paul made this point to the Roman believers: "But put on the Lord Jesus Christ [Yeshua the Messiah], and make no provision for the flesh, to fulfill its lusts" (Rom. 13:14).

Yes, Jesus Himself is our armor. His victory becomes ours as we allow Him to live His life through us. The believer's armor is simply Jesus in us living His life out of us; His victory over satan becomes our victory. This armor, as a description of the Lord, shows us how to live a victorious life and enter God's rest.

PROPHETIC SEASONAL ASPECT

The Feast of Tabernacles, consisting of Trumpets, Atonement, and Tabernacles, is the only one of the three feast seasons that has not yet been fulfilled in history. Both the feasts of Passover and Pentecost literally happened, as we have already learned. There is no reason for us to believe that the Feast of Tabernacles will not also be literally fulfilled in the future. In fact, it is already beginning to happen. We are living in this prophetic season.

The seasonal aspect of the Feast of Tabernacles relates to the great end-time events recorded by the prophets and in the Book of Revelation. Revelation opens with the apostle John hearing the voice of Jesus, which John likens to the sound of a trumpet. John writes, "I was in the Spirit on the Lord's Day, and I heard behind me a loud voice, as of a trumpet" (Rev. 1:10).

As we progress further into the Book of Revelation, we begin to see the literal fulfillment of the Feast of Trumpets. John writes, "After these things I looked, and behold, a door standing open in heaven. And the first voice which I heard was like a trumpet speaking with me, saying, "Come up here, and I will show you things which must take place after this" (Rev. 4:1).

John is then given a frightening vision of the use of trumpets to sound an alarm for warfare in the restoration of the nation of

Israel and the seven-year tribulation period described in Revelation 6 through 18.

The prophets in the Hebrew Bible described this period in terms of the blowing of trumpets for warfare. Joel wrote, "Blow the trumpet in Zion, and sound an alarm in My holy mountain! Let all the inhabitants of the land tremble; for the day of the Lord is coming, for it is at hand" (Joel 2:1). (See also Zephaniah 1:14-18.)

The ultimate fulfillment of the Feast of Trumpets is the return of Jesus, which is described in Revelation 19. It too is announced by the use of trumpets. John writes, "Then the seventh angel sounded: and there were loud voices in heaven, saying, "The kingdoms of the world have become the kingdoms of our Lord and of His Christ [Messiah], and He shall reign forever and ever!" (Rev. 11:15)

John goes on to say that when Jesus returns He will be coming to make war (see Rev. 19:11). He will crush all of His enemies and rule with a rod of iron over a Kingdom that will never end (see Rev. 19:15). Yes, Jesus is the trumpet of God and the horn of our salvation. He is our great Warrior-King who has defeated the enemies of God and God's people.

PERSONAL STUDY REVIEW

1. Describe how Jesus fulfilled the Feast of Trumpets.

2. How does the Feast of Trumpets as revealed in Jesus apply to our lives today?

3. Describe the seasonal aspect of the Feast of Trumpets.

4. Ask God to give you a personal encounter with Jesus as the spiritual reality of this feast.

ENDNOTES

1. For more information on the shofar and how it points to the Messiah, you may order the author's book online at www .rbooker.com. The book is titled *The Shofar: Ancient Sounds of the Messiah.*

2. "Roman Triumph," Wikipedia, accessed June 30, 2015, http:// en.wikipedia.org/wiki/Roman_triumph.

CHAPTER 7

ATONEMENT

One aspect of the Christian life that keeps many believers from entering God's rest is lack of repentance and failure to cope with trials. We all experience difficulties and failures in our walk with God. We must humble ourselves, repent of our sins, and seek the mercy of God when we fail to live up to His moral perfections. The Day of Atonement is a visual aid teaching us the necessity of entering God's rest and enjoying His presence. It represents the sixth step in our walk with God.

HISTORICAL BACKGROUND

The Lord gives us the following instructions concerning the Day of Atonement: "And the Lord spoke to 0Moses saying, 'Also the tenth day of this seventh month shall be the Day of Atonement. It shall be a holy convocation for you; you shall afflict your souls, and offer an offering made by fire to the Lord. And you shall do no work on that same day, for it is the Day of Atonement, to make atonement for you before the Lord your God.

"'For any person who is not afflicted in soul on that same day shall be cut off from his people. And any person who does any work on that same day, that person I will destroy from among his people. You shall do no manner of work; it shall be a statute forever throughout your generations in all your dwellings. It shall be to you a sabbath of solemn rest, and you shall afflict your souls; on the ninth day of the month at evening, from evening to evening, you shall celebrate your sabbath'" (Leviticus 23:26-32).

We learn from these Scriptures (and note on the chart) that the Day of Atonement was on the tenth day of the month of *Tishri*. This was the great day of national cleansing and repentance from sin. It was on this day that God judged the sins of the entire nation. In view of this, the Day of Atonement became known as the Day of Judgment.

The Day of Atonement was the one day in the year when the High Priest would go behind the veil into the Holy of Holies with the blood of the sacrifice and sprinkle it on the Mercy Seat. This offering of the innocent substitutionary sacrifice made possible the atonement for the sins of the nation. The word *atonement* means "to cover." On the great Day of Atonement, the sins of the nation were covered by the blood of the sacrifice. This dramatic procedure is described in detail in Leviticus 16 and in my book, *The Miracle of the Scarlet Thread*.

Because this was the Day of Judgment, it was a time of great soul affliction. It was a day of godly sorrow, godly repentance, and confession of sins. It was a time of mourning before God with a broken spirit and contrite heart. It is the only required day of fasting in the Bible (see Lev. 23:27,32; Jer. 36:6).

The Jews further believed that the final judgment and accounting of the soul would come on the Day of Atonement. On this day, the future of every individual would be sealed, and the gates of heaven would be closed. In light of this belief, the Jewish people perform many good deeds during the ten days between the Feast of Trumpets and the Day of Atonement. They say many profound prayers at the synagogue service seeking God's forgiveness and mercy.

This ten-day period is known as the "Awesome Days" or the "Ten Days of Repentance" as the people prepare themselves spiritually for the Day of Atonement. They express their concern and hope by greeting one another with the phrase, "May your name be inscribed in the Book of Life." It is a most solemn day.[1]

HOW JESUS FULFILLED THE FEAST

Jesus fulfilled the spiritual aspects of the Day of Atonement when He went into the heavenly holy of holies with His own blood He shed for the sins of the world. Believers have been forgiven and made clean once and for all by the blood of Messiah Jesus. His blood did what the blood of bulls and goats could never do for us. His blood didn't just cover our sins; it took them away to be remembered no more. Hallelujah!

We receive this great blessing of forgiveness once and for all when we repent of our sins and with a broken and contrite spirit, accept Jesus as the innocent substitutionary sacrifice who died in our place. At that moment, our future is sealed by the Holy Spirit, and our names are written in the Lamb's Book of Life. This is a finished work of redemption and salvation regarding our position before God.

Even though God has forgiven us of our sins, this does not mean that we do not need a continuous cleansing in our daily lives. We must judge our sins daily for the purpose of maintaining fellowship with the Lord. In this regard, the blood of Jesus purifies us so that we can have continuous fellowship with Him.

John spoke of this need with the following words: "If we say that we have fellowship with Him, and walk in darkness, we lie and do not practice the truth. But if we walk in the light as He is in the light, we have fellowship with one another, and the blood of Jesus Christ [Yeshua the Messiah] His Son cleanses us from all sin. If we say that we have no sin, we deceive ourselves, and the truth is not in us. If we confess our sins, He is faithful and just to forgive us our sins and to cleanse us from all unrighteousness" (1 John 1:6-9).

Human beings don't usually repent when all is going well for them. Because of this, God often allows us to go through various trials to test our faith and draw us closer to Him. Although God may not actually cause the difficulty in our lives, He will use it to purify our motives and actions so that we might turn from our sin and seek Him.

Jesus Himself experienced great trials. These were not for the purpose of cleansing and purifying Him, because Jesus did not need this. He was perfect. His trials were tests of obedience that forced Him to rely continually on His heavenly Father and seek Him through prayer and fasting.

Jesus desires to purify us by His Word. John 15:3 reads, "You are already clean because of the word which I have spoken to you." However, if we will not heed God's Word, Jesus will allow us to experience a "baptism in fire" to test our faith and bring us to repentance so that we might earnestly seek Him through prayer and fasting.

When John spoke of Jesus as the baptizer in the Holy Spirit, he also said that Jesus would baptize us with fire. John declared, "...I indeed baptize you with water; but One mightier than I is coming, whose sandal strap I am not worthy to loose. He will baptize you with the Holy Spirit and fire. His winnowing fan is in His hand, and He will thoroughly clean out His threshing floor, and gather the wheat into His barn; but the chaff He will burn with unquenchable fire" (Luke 3:16-17).

Jesus personally experienced this baptism in fire and promised that all who would follow Him would do likewise. We learn this from a conversation Jesus had with the mother of two of His disciples: "Then the mother of Zebedee's sons came to Him with her sons, kneeling down and asking something from Him. And He said to her, 'What do you wish?' She said to Him, 'Grant that these two sons of mine may sit, one on Your right hand and the other on the left, in Your kingdom.' But Jesus answered and said, 'You do not know what you ask. Are you able to drink the cup that I am about to drink, and be baptized with the baptism that I am baptized with?'

> *"They said to him, 'We are able.' So He said to them, 'You will indeed drink My cup, and be baptized with the baptism that I am baptized with; but to sit on My right hand and on My left is not Mine to give, but it is for those for whom it is prepared by My Father'"* (Matthew 20:20-23).

The woman in the story in Matthew wanted her two sons, James and John, to have the highest position in Jesus' Kingdom. However, she was not aware of the great price one must pay for such honor. Jesus said the price was to drink from the cup of baptism from which He was to drink. This cup was the great trial and testing He experienced a short time later, as well as the suffering He was to endure on the cross as He became our sin bearer and was separated from His Father in Heaven.

Just before His arrest, Jesus had gone to the Garden of Gethsemane to pray. This was to be His greatest time of testing. As He contemplated going to the cross, His soul became greatly distressed. He took Peter, James, and John with Him, hoping they would comfort Him.

Jesus said to them, "My soul is exceedingly sorrowful, even to death. Stay here and watch with Me" (Matt. 26:38). Then Jesus went a little further by Himself and began to cry out to God, "O My Father, if it is possible, let this cup pass from Me; nevertheless, not as I will, but as You will" (Matt. 26:39).

This was such a heavy burden for Jesus that His sweat "became like great drops of blood" (Luke 22:44). He cried out in desperation for God the Father to take the cup from Him, knowing all along this was not possible. Finally, He acknowledged the Father's will for His life and surrendered in total obedience to it. Jesus then went on to give His life in fulfillment of the spiritual reality of the Day of Atonement.

According to Leviticus 16, on the Day of Atonement, the High Priest was to present two goats before the Lord. He would then cast lots over the goats to determine which would be offered to the Lord and which would be led into the wilderness as the scapegoat. The goat on which the Lord's lot fell was offered as a sin offering. (See Leviticus 16:5-10.)

The religious leaders considered it a good omen if the lot marked "for the Lord" was drawn by the priest in his right hand. But according to traditional Jewish writings, for forty years prior to the destruction of the temple, the lot "for the Lord" appeared in his left hand. This bad omen caused great fear of impending doom.[2]

The High Priest tied a crimson wool thread around the horns of the scapegoat and sent him off into the wilderness accompanied by a priest. The goat was escorted for twelve miles to a designated place, where the priest pushed the goat bearing Israel's sins over a cliff . A portion of the crimson thread was attached to the door of the temple before the goat was sent into the wilderness. When the goat was pushed off the cliff and died, the thread on the door at the temple was said to turn from red to white. This was a divine sign to the people that God had accepted their sacrifice and their sins were forgiven.

This sign was based on Isaiah 1:18, which says, "though your sins are as scarlet, they will be as white as snow; though they are red like crimson, they will be like wool." Rabbinic writings tell us that for forty years prior to the destruction of the temple, the thread stopped turning white.[3]

Further signs of doom were that the westernmost light on the Temple candelabra would not burn. This was a bad omen that the light of the Temple was going to be extinguished. Furthermore, the Temple doors would open by themselves. The rabbis saw this as a sign that the Temple was going to be destroyed by fire as God's judgment for their ungodliness. This was based on their understanding of Zechariah 11:1, which says, "Open your doors, O Lebanon, that fire may devour your cedars."[4]

The obvious significance of these signs is that they began to appear forty years prior to the destruction of the temple. This was when Jesus was crucified. It was a most dramatic way for God to demonstrate that Jesus was the ultimate human reality of the Day of Atonement. His death provided the once-and-for-all forgiveness for sin. Thank You, Jesus!

PERSONAL APPLICATION

Whatever Jesus experienced in His flesh while on earth, we who are His followers will experience in our inner self. Jesus was crucified for our sins. Our response is to die to self, take up our cross, and follow Him. Jesus was buried with our sins. Our response is to put off the old man of sin. Jesus was resurrected from the dead. Likewise, we who were dead in our trespasses and sins have been raised from our spiritual grave to walk in newness of life.

Jesus was filled with the Holy Spirit, enabling Him to minister in the power of God. We too must be filled with the Holy Spirit for the same purpose. After Jesus was filled with the Holy Spirit, He immediately encountered spiritual warfare and many trials to test His faith. Likewise, when we become filled with the Holy Spirit, we encounter spiritual warfare and great trials beyond any dimension we have previously known. This is a great challenge, and only the strong in the Lord who understand spiritual warfare persevere. This is one reason why weak, carnal, cultural Christians do not experience the blessings of God. They are unwilling and/or unable to walk with Him to Tabernacles. God will help us if we will allow Him to work this in our lives.

Jesus was also judged for our sins. Therefore, we must judge ourselves or He will chasten us so that we will not be condemned with the world. Paul explains this to us, "For if we would judge ourselves, we would not be judged. But when we are judged, we are chastened by the Lord, that we may not be condemned with the world" (1 Cor. 11:31-32).

As long as we are on this planet, until Jesus returns, we are going to have trials. God uses them to humble us, to test our faith, and to show us the real condition of our heart. Moses understood this and wrote, "And you shall remember that the Lord your God led you all the way these forty years in the wilderness, to humble you and test you, to know what was in your heart, whether you would keep His commandment" (Deut. 8:2).

Peter wrote, "Beloved, do not think it strange concerning the fiery trial which is to try you, as though some strange thing happened to you...the time has come for judgment to begin at the house of God...Therefore let those who suffer according to the will of God [for righteousness sake] commit their souls to Him in doing good, as to a faithful Creator" (1 Pet. 4:12, 17, 19).

Jesus did not die to save us from trials and problems, but He will help us overcome our trials and problems as we seek His face and repent, when necessary. Our response to trials and problems is not to run from them or pretend they don't exist, but to commit our soul to God, who is a faithful Creator. He will never allow us to have a trial so great that He will not give us the grace to overcome it. (See First Corinthians 10:13 and Second Corinthians 12:9-10.)

Peter explains, "In this you greatly rejoice, though now for a little while, if need be, you have been grieved by various trials, that the genuineness of your faith, being much more precious than gold that perishes, though it is tested by fire, may be found to praise, honor, and glory at the revelation of Jesus Christ [Yeshua the Messiah]" (1 Peter 1:6-7).

We can learn some very helpful points from Peter regarding the trials of our faith. First of all, he says we will only have a trial "if need be." In other words, God will not allow us to experience a difficult trial of our faith unless He sees some value in it for our life.

There is a purpose in every trial we face. Therefore, when experiencing a trial, we should seek to understand what lesson God has for us. We should take our eyes off the circumstances and try to view the situation from an eternal perspective. While this is easier said than done, God will help us overcome these difficult times in our lives through praise and worship, meditating on His Word, fellowship with other believers, etc.

Peter next encourages us by saying the difficulty we face will be only for a "little while." It won't last forever. Now that's good news. Once we respond in the way that God desires, the trial will pass. We determine how long the trial will last by the way in which we respond. If we become angry with God because of our circumstances or try to run from them, we actually prolong our difficulty. But if we seek God through prayer and fasting, and with a broken and contrite spirit, the trial will soon pass.

Peter then says that we will have "various" trials. Sometimes it seems as if our whole world is falling apart. Everything seems to be going wrong. This does not necessarily mean that we are living in sin or that God is punishing us. It could very well be just the normal pressures of life that pile up from time to time. God will use them in our lives to develop His character in us, if we will allow Him to do this deeper work in us.

Next, Peter points out the obvious: going through a trial can be a very grievous and stressful experience. To acknowledge this does not mean that we lack faith, or that we are not trusting God. It merely means we are facing the situation realistically. We are being human and honest. The good news is that we do not have to carry our burdens alone. We can give them to God through prayer and thanksgiving (see 1 Pet. 5:7).

Finally, Peter states that the purpose of trials is to test the genuineness of our faith. He compares this test to the process used in purifying gold. When a miner finds gold, the ore contains a lot of impurities. The miner must "test" the gold for the purpose of separating it from the impurities. The way he does this is by putting the gold in a crucible, which he places over a fiery furnace. The heat from the fire causes the impurities to rise to the top of the crucible. The miner then skims off the impurities and looks down into the material in the crucible. He cannot see if there is more impure material because it will be at the bottom of the crucible.

However, if the miner cannot see a clear reflection of his image, he knows there are more impurities at the bottom that need to be removed. The way he removes them is by turning up the fire. This causes more impurities to rise to the top, and once again, the miner skims them off from the surface. He repeats this process until he is able to see a clear reflection of his image in the remaining material in the crucible. At this point, he knows he has separated out all the impurities.

This illustration helps us to understand why we have trials and how God uses them to test our faith. The prophets spoke of God as a refiner who would burn out the moral and spiritual impurities from our lives. Malachi said, "He will sit as a refiner and a purifier of silver; He will purify the sons of Levi, and purge them as gold and silver, that they may offer to the Lord an offering in righteousness" (Mal. 3:3). (See also Isaiah 1:25.)

God desires that His children be conformed to His image. So like the old miner, the Lord tests our faith. He uses the trials of life for the purpose of bringing to the top of our attention those things hidden deep in our hearts. These hidden things are below the surface of our knowledge. We don't even know they are there. The Lord then skims them off as we pray, repent, and seek His face. He repeats this process, making the fiery trial hotter if necessary, until there is nothing left of us but Him. That glorious outcome makes the trials of life worthwhile.

Job was a man who suffered great trials. Yet he found comfort in knowing that God was working in his life. Job understood the refining process God often allows us to experience. Job said, "Look, I go forward, but He is not there, and backward, but I cannot perceive Him; when He works on the left hand, I cannot behold Him; when He turns to the right hand, I cannot see Him. But He knows the way that I take; when He has tested me, I shall come forth as gold" (Job 23:8-10).

You may be going through a difficult trial in your life. Perhaps you cannot sense God's presence, but He is there. He promised to never leave you nor forsake you (see Heb. 13:5). He promised to make a way for you to overcome your burden (see 1 Cor. 10:13).

God knows what is going on in your life. He knows what is best for you from an eternal perspective. He knows what you can handle and what would overwhelm you. He knows what He is doing in your life. He promises that all things will work together for your good (see Rom. 8:28). Take comfort in these words, "When He has tried you, you shall come forth as gold."

PROPHETIC SEASONAL ASPECT

The prophetic season of the Day of Atonement points to the return of Jesus to judge the earth. This future event will literally be fulfilled on the final great Day of Atonement.

God established every fiftieth year as a Year of Jubilee in the Jewish administration of time (see Lev. 27). This was a special year when all the prisoners were set free, property was returned to its original owner, and the land rested, without being worked. This was the year for proclaiming liberty throughout the land. It was a time of great rejoicing.

The Year of Jubilee begins on the Day of Atonement. It points to the great Year of Jubilee when Messiah Jesus will come to earth to judge the world. Then, God's people will be set free once and for all from the trials and burdens of life. The rule of earth will be restored to the godly, and there will be rest in the land. This will be a day of mourning for those who will be judged but a day of rejoicing for believers.

The prophet Zechariah was speaking of the future literal fulfillment of the Day of Atonement when he wrote these words, "And I will pour on the house of David and on the inhabitants of Jerusalem the Spirit of grace and supplication; then they will look on Me whom they have pierced; they will mourn for Him as one mourns for his only son, and grieve for Him as one grieves for a firstborn. In that day there shall be a great mourning in Jerusalem, like the mourning at Hadad Rimmon in the plain of Megiddo. And the land shall mourn, every family by itself, the family of the house of David by itself, and their wives by themselves; the family of Nathan by itself, and their wives by themselves; the family of the house of Levi by itself, and their wives by themselves, the family of Shimei by itself, and their wives by themselves; all the families that remain, every family by itself, and their wives by themselves" (Zech. 12:10-14).

Zechariah added this further word, "In that day a fountain shall be opened for the house of David and for the inhabitants of Jerusalem, for sin and for uncleanness. 'It shall be in that day,' says the Lord of hosts, 'that I will cut off the names of the idols from the land, and they shall no longer be remembered. I will also cause the prophets and the unclean spirit to depart from the land....' 'And it shall come to pass in all the land,' says the Lord, 'that two-thirds in it shall be cut off and die, but one third shall be left in it: I will bring the one-third through the fire, will refine them as silver is refined, and test them as gold is tested. They will call on My name, and I will answer them. I will say, "This is My people"; and each one will say, "The Lord is my God"'" (Zech. 13:1-2, 8-9).

Jesus also referred to this time when speaking about His return to the earth. He said, "Immediately after the tribulation of those days the sun will be darkened, and the moon will not give its light; the stars will fall from heaven, and the powers of the heavens will be shaken. Then the sign of the Son of Man will appear in heaven, and then all the tribes of the earth will mourn, and they will see the Son of Man coming on the clouds of heaven with power and great glory. And He will send His angels with a great sound of a trumpet, and they will gather together His elect from the four winds, from one end of heaven to the other" (Matt. 24:29-31).

John said these words in the Book of Revelation, "Behold, He is coming with clouds, and every eye will see Him, even they who pierced Him. And all the tribes of the earth will mourn because of Him. Even so, Amen" (Rev. 1:7).

John also had the great privilege of writing about Jesus' literal fulfillment of the Day of Atonement. He explains, "Now I saw heaven opened, and behold, a white horse. And He who sat on him was called Faithful and True, and in righteousness He judges and makes war. His eyes were like a flame of fire, and on His head were many crowns. He had a name written that no one knew except Himself. He was clothed with a robe dipped in blood, and His name is called The Word of God.

> *"And the armies in heaven, clothed in fine linen, white and clean, followed Him on white horses. Now out of His mouth goes a sharp sword, that with it He should strike the nations. And He Himself will rule them with a rod of iron. He Himself treads the winepress of the fierceness and wrath of Almighty God. And He has on His robe and on His thigh a*

name written: KING OF KINGS AND LORD OF LORDS" (Revelation 19:11-16).

PERSONAL STUDY REVIEW

1. Describe how Jesus fulfills the Feast of Atonement.

2. How does the Feast of Atonement as revealed in Jesus apply to our lives today?

3. Describe the seasonal aspect of the Feast of Atonement.

4. Ask God to give you a personal encounter with Jesus as the spiritual reality of this feast.

ENDNOTES

1. "The Book of Life," Jews for Jesus, accessed June 30, 2015, http://jewsforjesus.org/publications/issues/v01-n01/bookoflife.

2. Scott Sekulow, "Yom Kippur," The Messianic Hour, Yom Kippur in Yeshua's Time, accessed June 30, 2015, http://www.israelsharvest.com/yom_kippur.html.

3. Ibid.

4. Ibid.

CHAPTER 8

TABERNACLES

The last feast God gave the Hebrews to observe was the Feast of Tabernacles (*Succot* in Hebrew). It was also called the Feast of Ingathering because it was at the end of the harvest season, and the Feasts of Booths because the Hebrews slept in booths or shelters during the feast (see Exod. 23:16; Deut. 16:16).

The Feast of Tabernacles celebrated the final ingathering of the harvest God had blessed the people with for the year. The fruit of the land had been reaped, so the people could rest from their harvest labors. It was a time of great rejoicing. In fact, it was such a joyous occasion that the rabbis said the person who had not been to Jerusalem during the Feast of Tabernacles didn't know what rejoicing really meant.[1]

Because the Feast of Tabernacles was the last of the seven feasts, it completed the religious season. The number seven in the Bible represents completion. We learn from this that the Feast of Tabernacles represents the completed or finished work of God in both this present age in which we live and the lives of individual believers. It corresponds to the seventh step in our walk with God to reach spiritual maturity and rest in our souls.

This is not the same as sinless perfection. We will never achieve this until Jesus returns. It is, however, a level of maturity to which we can grow, learning not only to rest in God for who He is but also to be content in whatever circumstances we find ourselves.

Paul recognized this condition in his own life. He was not perfect, but he had matured to a place of rest in God. He expressed this in the following way, "Not that I have already attained, or am already perfected; but I press on, that I may lay hold of that for which Christ [Messiah] Jesus has also laid hold of me. Brethren, I do not count myself to have apprehended; but one thing I do, forgetting those things which are behind and reaching forward to those things which are ahead, I press toward the goal for the prize of the upward call of God in Christ [Messiah] Jesus.

> *"Not that I speak in regard to need, for I have learned in whatever state I am, to be content: I know how to be abased, and I know how to abound. Everywhere and in all things I have learned both to be full and to be hungry, both to abound and to suffer need. I can do all things through Christ [Messiah] who strengthens me"* (Philippians 3:12-14; 4:11-13).

HISTORICAL BACKGROUND

Let's now read the instructions the Lord gave concerning the Feast of Tabernacles, "Then the Lord spoke to Moses saying: 'Speak to the children of Israel, saying, "The fifteenth day of this seventh month shall be the Feast of Tabernacles for seven days to the Lord. On the first day there shall be a holy convocation. You shall do no customary work on it. For seven days you shall offer an offering made by fire to the Lord. On the eighth day you shall have a holy convocation, and you shall offer an offering made by fire to the Lord. It is a sacred assembly, and you shall do no customary work on it"'" (Lev. 23:33-36).

God then repeated the command and gave further instructions, "Also on the fifteenth day of the seventh month, when you have gathered in the fruit of the land, you shall keep the feast of the Lord for seven days; on the first day there shall be a sabbath-rest, and on the eighth day a sabbath-rest. And you shall take for yourselves on the first day the fruit of beautiful trees, branches of palm trees, the boughs of leafy trees, and willows of the brook; and you shall rejoice before the Lord for seven days. You shall keep it as a feast to the Lord for seven days in the year. It shall be a statute forever in your generations. You shall celebrate it in the seventh month.

"You shall dwell in booths for seven days. All who are native Israelites shall dwell in booths, that your generations may know that I made the children of Israel dwell in booths when I brought them out of the land of Egypt: I am the Lord your God" (Lev. 23:39-43). (See also Numbers 29 for a description of sacrifices that were offered to the Lord at this feast.)

We learn from this text that the Feast of Tabernacles began on the 15th of *Tishri* and lasted through the 21st. Then on the 22nd (the eighth day), there was a special Sabbath, which was a day of rest characterized by much rejoicing.

The Feast of Tabernacles had two aspects associated with it. First, it looked back to the forty years when the Jews wandered in the desert living in shelters or tabernacles. They were always to be reminded that the wanderings of their forefathers were brought about by unbelief and disobedience, but they were only temporary. Even during their wanderings, God was in their midst, providing for their every need and eventually bringing them into the land of rest He had promised them.

As a constant reminder, God commanded the Hebrews to build booths or shelters to live in during this feast. So every year at the Feast of Tabernacles, the Hebrews would gather the necessary wood and branches and build a shelter in which they would live during the feast. Many Jews still do this today.

But the Feast of Tabernacles also had a forward look. The shelter was loosely constructed so that the Hebrews could see through its roof into the heavens. This would remind them that they were pilgrims passing through this life and that God had an even greater rest for them in the future when He would come and live among them permanently.

This final rest was the hope of their ancestor Abraham. The writer of Hebrews referred to this and said, "By faith Abraham obeyed when he was called to go out to the place which he would receive as an inheritance; and he went out, not knowing where he was to go. By faith he dwelt in the land of promise as in a foreign country, dwelling in tents with Isaac and Jacob, the heirs with him of the same promise. For he waited for the city which has foundations, whose builder and maker is God" (Heb. 11:8-10).

HOW JESUS FULFILLED THE FEAST

Jesus is the ultimate tabernacle or dwelling place of God in human flesh (see John 1:14; Col. 2:9). God dwells in our midst through Jesus, who gives us His Spirit in our hearts (see Matt. 18:20). Jesus will fulfill the Feast of Tabernacles at His second coming. There will be a literal rest for the earth and all of its inhabitants. Until then, we can know rest in our souls.

On one occasion Jesus said, "Come to Me, all you who labor and are heavy laden, and I will give you rest. Take My yoke upon you and learn from Me, for I am gentle and lowly in heart, and you will find rest for your souls. For My yoke is easy and My burden is light" (Matt. 11:28-30).

Jesus claimed that we could find rest in God through Him. Many believers seek God's rest by working for God or trying to get something from God. Others look to symbols that point to God for assurance and comfort. But God Himself is our rest through a personal relationship with Jesus.

You see, Jesus doesn't give us life; He is our life. He doesn't give us peace; He is our peace. He doesn't give us love; He is love. He is in Himself all that we need. What we try to get from God are simply manifestations of God's own life.

Many believers never enter God's rest because they seek things from Jesus rather than Jesus Himself. They seek blessings rather than the One who blesses. Jesus doesn't give us blessings; He Himself is our blessing. He is all that we could ever need, want, or hope for in His person.

Jesus Himself is our rest. His rest is available for us when we allow Him to fully dwell in our midst as Lord and Master of our soul. This becomes a reality to us by the Holy Spirit, through whom the life of Jesus flows to us and through us.

There were two Jewish rituals associated with the Feast of Tabernacles that dramatically illustrated the difference between the ritual that pointed to Jesus and the reality of Jesus the person.

The first was the ritual of the pouring of water. This took place on the last day of the Feast of Tabernacles. The day was called in Hebrew *Hoshanah Rabbah,* which means the "Day of the Great Hosanna." This Hebrew phrase translates into English as "save now" or "deliver us!"[2] The Day of the Great Hosanna was the day when the Jews would pray for rain and God's salvation through the Messiah.

The ritual of the pouring of the water had both a physical and spiritual significance. The rainy season was about to begin, and the Jews needed the rain to soften the ground for plowing. In view of this, they made a special thanksgiving offering to God for the rain He was going to send. The spiritual significance pointed to the coming of the Messiah who would give them the living waters of His Spirit.

As part of the ritual proceeding, a certain priest would draw water from the Pool of Siloam with a golden pitcher. He would then come to the altar at the temple where the High Priest would take the pitcher and pour the water into a basin at the foot of the altar. As this was taking place, the priests blew their trumpets, and the Levites and all the people waved palm branches while singing to the Lord.

About the time the water was being poured they were singing and praising God with these words from Isaiah, "Therefore with joy you will draw water from the wells of salvation" (Isa. 12:3).

They also sought the Lord from Isaiah 44:3, which reads, "For I will pour water on him who is thirsty, and floods on the dry ground; I will pour My Spirit on your descendants, and My blessing on your offspring." This was the most joyous day of the celebration, and the pouring of the water was the most joyous moment of the day.[3]

Jesus was there to keep the feast in obedience to the Torah. Just as the fervor of the celebration reached it peak at the pouring of water, Jesus made a bold declaration. John was an eyewitness to it and told the story, "On the last day, that great day of the feast, Jesus stood and cried out, saying, 'If anyone thirsts, let him come to Me and drink. He who believes in Me, as the Scripture has said, out of his heart will flow rivers of living water.' But this He spoke concerning the Spirit, whom those believing in Him would receive; for the Holy Spirit was not yet given, because Jesus was not yet glorified" (John 7:37-39).

With this statement, Jesus was saying, "Look unto Me and be saved now. I am the 'Great Hosanna.' I am your salvation. I will give the living waters of the Holy Spirit to all who will receive Me as the true tabernacle of God."

The other ritual was the lighting of the temple. Tens of thousands of pilgrims who had come to Jerusalem to keep the feast crowded into the temple area. Many carried a lighted torch so that the entire city was illuminated for miles. This too had a physical and spiritual significance.

Plenty of sunshine was needed along with the rain to have a successful agricultural season. The Jews thanked God for the sun that was necessary for the life of the harvest. They also recognized that God Himself was the true light (see Ps. 27:1) who would give them spiritual light and life through the Messiah.[4]

It was during this occasion that Jesus made another bold statement that most assuredly got their attention. John records it for us, "Then Jesus spoke to them again, saying, 'I am the light of the world. He who follows Me shall not walk in darkness, but have the light of life'" (John 8:12).

At both of these very special festival events, Jesus proclaimed in a clear and powerful way that He was the reality to which the feast pointed. While many believed in Him, Jesus was rejected by the political and religious leaders, the establishment. The result has been that the Jewish people have been restless wanderers for the past 2,000 years, not only as a people, but in their souls as well. This is about to change—and is already begun.

PERSONAL APPLICATION

There is a rest for our souls today as well as a future heavenly rest. The writer of Hebrews explains what we must do to enter this rest. He begins by reminding us that God had a rest for the Jews, but they failed to embrace it. He says, "...Today, if you will hear His voice, do not harden your hearts as in the rebellion, in the day of trial in the wilderness, where your fathers tested Me, tried Me, and saw My works forty years. Therefore I was angry with that generation, and said, 'They always go astray in their heart, and they have not known My ways.' So I swore in My wrath, 'They shall not enter My rest'" (Heb. 3:7-11).

It was God's desire to lead the Hebrews into their promised land of rest. But an entire generation didn't make it. They died in the wilderness because of unbelief and disobedience brought about by a hard heart against God (see Heb. 3:16-19). The writer of Hebrews then warns us against the same problem. He says, "Beware, brethren, lest there be in any of you an evil heart of unbelief in departing from the living God; but exhort one another daily, while it is called 'Today,' lest any of you be hardened through the deceitfulness of sin. For we have become partakers of Christ [Messiah] if we hold the beginning of our confidence steadfast to the end, while it is said: 'Today, if you will hear His voice, do not harden your hearts as in the rebellion'" (Heb. 3:12-15).

Finally, as if to press the point, we are further exhorted by another reminder, "For who, having heard, rebelled? Indeed, was it not all who came out of Egypt, led by Moses?...And to whom did He swear that they would not enter His rest, but to those who did not obey? So we see that they could not enter in because of unbelief" (Heb. 3:16-19).

The Hebrews who came out of Egypt and died in the wilderness were saved, but they did not enter God's rest. (See Numbers 14:19-23.) God's rest is not "dying and going to Heaven." It is living in the fullness of God's life here and now. It is walking in His peace, His power, and His rest as pictured in the feasts.

In the Bible, Egypt symbolizes the world system. The Promised Land represents God's rest. The wilderness lies in between. When a person accepts Jesus as Lord and Savior, God delivers him or her out of a type of spiritual Egypt. Believers come out of spiritual Egypt the moment they receive Jesus into their life. But Egypt (the ways of the world) doesn't always come out of the believer, at least not for a while.

Like the Hebrews of old, we believers will not enjoy God's rest in our life unless we walk with Him in loving trust and obedience.

This involves taking the seven steps presented in this book. While all believers will experience God's final rest in Heaven, some will miss it in their present life.

The Lord desires for us to enter His rest in our soul in this present life through a daily walk with Him. The first step is to accept Jesus as the Passover Lamb who died for our sins. At the moment we receive Jesus into our life, we experience a spiritual birth which is so dramatic, Jesus spoke of it as being born again (see John 3:1-8). We then die to our old self-life (Egypt in us) by putting off the old man and putting on the new man (see Col. 3:9-10). These two steps symbolized by the Feast of Unleavened Bread and Firstfruits, are necessary to produce the character of Jesus in us.

We might think of believers who have taken these first steps as Passover Christians. They have peace with God and the peace of God. But they have not fully experienced the power of God. They must go on to the fourth step: Pentecost. Your church tradition and doctrines may not teach or believe that this encounter with God is for us today. I have no desire to debate church doctrines. I only ask this simple question, "Do you have spiritual power in your life?" If not, you need this encounter with the Living God.

The Pentecostal experience enables the believer to be an effective witness and to minister in the power of the Holy Spirit. But the Pentecostal believer is only halfway to God's rest. He or she must also go on to become a Tabernacle Christian. We must all learn how to conduct spiritual warfare, repent of our sins, and overcome the trials of our faith. As we take each of these steps in trust and obedience to God, we will enjoy His divine rest in our souls.

PROPHETIC SEASONAL ASPECT

The Feast of Tabernacles represents the 1,000-year reign of Messiah Jesus on earth. This period of time is known as the Millennium, from the Latin words *milli* (one thousand) and *annum* (year).

It will be a time of great rejoicing. The curse of sin will be almost completely lifted and satan bound so that both the earth and its inhabitants will enjoy the rest of God.

This 1,000-year reign of Jesus is the subject of the 20th chapter of the Book of Revelation. We read in the first five verses, "Then I saw an angel coming down from heaven, having the key to the bottomless pit and a great chain in his hand. He laid hold of the dragon, that serpent of old, who is the Devil and Satan, and bound him for a thousand years; and he cast him into the bottomless pit, and shut him up, and set a seal on him, so that he should deceive the nations no more till the thousand years were finished. But after these things he must be released for a little while....

> *"Then I saw the souls of those who had been beheaded for their witness to Jesus and for the word of God, who had not worshipped the beast or his image, and had not received his mark on their foreheads or on their hands. And they lived and reigned with Christ [Messiah] for a thousand years. But the rest of the dead did not live again until the thousand years were finished. This is the first resurrection"* (Revelation 20:1-6).

This seasonal rest of the Feast of Tabernacles is described in detail throughout the Bible, but particularly by the prophets in the Hebrew Scriptures. It is the utopia for which man has so desperately striven—but never achieved—because he has tried to establish it without God.

Isaiah was looking forward to this time when he wrote, "Therefore the redeemed for the Lord shall return, and come with singing unto Zion; and everlasting joy shall be upon their head: they shall obtain gladness and joy; and sorrow and mourning shall flee away" (Isa. 51:11 KJV).

The prophet Zechariah said that when Messiah comes, all nations will go to Jerusalem to worship the Lord and celebrate this feast: "And it shall come to pass, that everyone who is left of all the nations which came against Jerusalem shall go up from year to year to worship the King, the Lord of hosts, and to keep the Feast of Tabernacles" (Zech. 14:16).

In anticipation of this glorious time of rejoicing on the earth, Christians have been celebrating the Feast of Tabernacles in Jerusalem since 1980. It is a time of great rejoicing. Each year approximately 5,000 believers from 100 nations go up to Jerusalem to "keep the Feast." You see, it is not a "Jewish Feast"; it is a "Jesus Feast." It is a Feast of the Lord.

Along with my wife, Peggy, I have taken tour groups to Israel to celebrate the Feast of Tabernacles for over 20 years. I was honored to be a speaker at the Christian celebration of the Feast in Jerusalem for 18 years. We meet in the day for seminars and then gather at night for glorious times of praise, pageantry, and celebration with our brothers and sisters from around the world.

Perhaps the most memorable time at the Feast of Tabernacles is the Jerusalem Parade. The 5,000 Christians join with another 5,000 Israelis representing different groups for a joyful and emotional parade through the streets of Jerusalem. Tens of thousands of Israelis line the streets and greet us with an incredible love and joy that is literally indescribable. The parade is such an overwhelming experience; people cannot contain their tears of joy as they reach out to one another in love and friendship. I long for the day when Messiah will come, and we will all be with Him at the Feast of Tabernacles in Jerusalem.[5]

As wonderful as this time will be for the earth and all its inhabitants, it is still not the final rest that God has for us. We learn from Leviticus that there was a special Sabbath on the eighth day (the 22nd). This was a day of great rejoicing and corresponds to the new heaven and new earth.

John explains, "Now I saw a new heaven and a new earth, for the first heaven and the first earth had passed away. Also there was no more sea. Then I, John, saw the holy city, New Jerusalem, coming down out of heaven from God, prepared as a bride adorned for her husband. And I heard a loud voice from heaven saying, 'Behold the tabernacle of God is with men, and He will dwell with them, and they shall be His people, and God Himself will be with them and be their God. And God will wipe away every tear from their eyes; there shall be no more death, nor sorrow, nor crying; and there shall be no more pain, for the former things have passed away.'

> *"Then He who sat on the throne said, 'Behold I make all things new.' And He said to me, 'Write, for these words are true and faithful.' And He said to me, 'It is done! I am the Alpha and the Omega, the Beginning and the End. I will give of the fountain of the water of life freely to him who thirsts'"* (Revelation 21:1-6).

In these verses, John explains that God will transfer His home from Heaven to earth. God will dwell in our midst and pull down the curtain on the closing act of human history. Then eternity will begin with God coming to live in the midst of His people. This is the final rest for which all believers are waiting.

Finally, John gives the last word, "And He showed me a pure river of water of life, clear as crystal, proceeding from the throne of God and of the Lamb. In the middle of its street, and on either side of the river, was the tree of life, which bore twelve fruits, each tree yielding its fruit every month. And the leaves of the tree were for the healing of the nations. And there shall be no more curse, but the throne of God and of the Lamb shall be in it, and His servants shall serve Him. They shall see His face, and His name shall be on their foreheads. And there shall be no night there: they need no lamp nor light of the sun, for the Lord God gives them light. And they shall reign forever and ever" (Rev. 22:1-5).

PERSONAL STUDY REVIEW

1. Describe how Jesus fulfilled the Feast of Tabernacles.

2. How does the Feast of Tabernacles as revealed in Jesus apply to our lives today?

3. Describe the seasonal aspect of the Feast of Tabernacles.

4. Ask God to give you a personal encounter with Jesus as the spiritual reality of this feast.

ENDNOTES

1. John J. Parsons, "Hoshana Rabba: The Great Salvation," Hebrew for Christians, accessed June 30, 2015, http://www.hebrew4christians.com/Holidays/Fall_Holidays/Hoshana_Rabbah/hoshana_rabbah.html.

2. Ibid.

3. Ibid.

4. Rob Phillips, "Jesus in the Feasts of Israel: Tabernacles (Sukkot)," OnceDelivered.net, September 07, 2008, http://oncedelivered.wordpress.com/2008/09/07/jesus-in-the-feasts-of-israel-tabernacles-sukkot/.

5. If this stirs your heart and you would like information about our Feast tours, please contact us, and we would be happy to discuss this with you.

CHAPTER 9

PURIM

At this point in this book, we have studied the biblical Feasts of the Lord. We have learned their historical background, how they point to Jesus, and how they apply to our world and lives today. In this and the next chapter, we will study two additional Jewish holidays that are not Feasts of the Lord but are very important to the Jewish people.

These are national holidays that celebrate the victory of the Jewish people over their enemies who wanted to destroy them. Without these victories, the Jewish people would have perished from the face of the earth. This would mean that the God of the Bible is not the true God and the Bible is a lie. It would also mean that Jesus Christ (Yeshua the Messiah) would not have been born.

Furthermore, as we will learn, the New Testament tells us that Jesus celebrated these holidays. For these reasons Christians should certainly want to know about these two very important national holidays—Purim and Hanukkah. We will learn about Purim in this chapter and Hanukkah in the following chapter.

HISTORICAL BACKGROUND

The background for Purim is found in the book of Esther. This book tells the wonderful story of how the Jewish Queen Esther interceded for her people to save them from the plot of Haman, a wicked man who wanted to destroy the Jews. The story of Esther takes place in the period of Persian rule when Ahasuerus was king. This was approximately 485–465 B.C. This king is also thought to be King Xerxes I, who succeeded Darius I. Xerxes is the Greek form of his Persian name. He ruled for twenty years over a vast empire that included 127 provinces that stretched from India to Ethiopia.

The king lived in the Persian capital of Shushan. During his rule, there were a number of Jews who still lived in Babylon under Persian sovereignty, even though Cyrus allowed them to return to Israel approximately fifty years earlier (see Ezra 1:1-4). It is certainly worth noting that the Jews in Persia would not have been in danger of annihilation if they had returned to Israel.

The historians tell us that Ahasuerus ruled over his empire with absolute power. He had a violent, unpredictable temperament and an uncontrolled lust for pleasure. When offered a large sum of money toward the expenses of a military campaign, King Ahasuerus was so impressed by the loyalty of the donor, he returned the funds along with a present expressing his gratitude. However, when the same donor requested exemption from military service for one of his sons, the king had the son cut into two pieces and marched his army between them.

When he was defeated in a battle, the king pacified himself by offering a prize to anyone who thought of some new indulgence that pleased the king. He was just the sort of man to dethrone his queen for refusing to expose herself before his drunken guests.

In the third year of his rule (482 B.C.), King Ahasuerus threw a party that lasted for 180 days. After this party was over, the king had another party for the people who lived in the capitol. Queen Vashti also made a feast for the women in the royal palace. On the seventh day of the party, the king commanded his seven eunuchs to bring Queen Vashti to him so he could show off her beauty to the people and officials. Much to everyone's shock, the queen refused to come.

The Book of Esther tells the story, "But Queen Vashti refused to come at the king's command brought by his eunuchs; therefore the king was furious, and his anger burned within him" (Esther 1:12).

The English translation really doesn't communicate to the reader what should be obvious. The king and his male friends were having a drunken orgy and the king wanted to publicly demonstrate his manliness with the queen whose name means "beautiful woman." To her credit, if not to her good judgment, the queen refused to participate. It was a gross breach of Persian etiquette to demand the queen immodestly display herself before a vast company of half-intoxicated revelers. Archaeologists have confirmed that this very "palace of iniquity" was destroyed by fire within 30 years of the time of Esther. French archaeologists have uncovered its remains.[1]

Now the king could not allow his queen to get away with such rebellion. This was before the days of women's lib. What would his male friends think? If the queen got away with such open rebellion, then every woman in the kingdom might get the idea that she "had a mind of her own."

The king called together his counselors, who advised the king to issue a royal decree that Vashti would no longer be queen and that the king would give her position to another more worthy, "If it pleases the king, let a royal decree go out from him, and let it be recorded in the laws of the Persians and the Medes, so that it will not be altered, that Vashti shall come no more before King Ahasuerus; and let the king give her royal position to another who is better than she" (Esther 1:19).

The wise counselors suggested a new queen be found for the king. Beautiful young virgins from all the provinces of his kingdom were gathered that the king might choose his new queen: "Then the king's servants who attended him said: 'Let beautiful young virgins be sought for the king; and let the king appoint officers in all the provinces of the kingdom, that they may gather all the beautiful young virgins to Shushan the citadel, into the women's quarters, under the custody of Hegai the king's eunuch, custodian of the women. And let beauty preparations be given them. Then let the young woman who pleases the king be queen instead of Vashti.' This thing pleased the king, and he did so" (Esther 2:2-4).

A young woman name Esther was chosen as one of the virgins to be taken to the palace. Esther's Hebrew name is *Hadassah,* meaning "myrtle." Her Persian name means "star." For the next 12 months, Esther lived what must have seemed like a dream. She was given an allowance and servants to attend her every need. She was pampered for six months with oil of myrrh and six months with perfumes and other cosmetics. Mary Kay would have given anything for the marketing rights to these beauty products.

When her year of preparation was over, Esther was taken before the king. He chose her over all the other women, put the royal crown on her head, and made her queen. The king did not know that Esther had Jewish blood flowing in her veins. She was raised by her cousin, Mordecai, a Benjamite who feared the Lord. Esther 2:16-17 reads, "So Esther was taken to King Ahasuerus, into his royal palace, in the tenth month, which is the month of Tebeth, in the seventh year of his reign. The king loved Esther more than all the other women, and she obtained grace and favor in his sight more than all the virgins; so he set the royal crown upon her head and made her queen instead of Vashti."

While Mordecai sat within the king's gate, two of the king's eunuchs, Bigthan and Teresh, sought to kill the king. Mordecai learned of the plot and told it to Esther, who informed the king in Mordecai's name. Both plotters where hanged on gallows. While the episode was noted in the king's records, Mordecai received no recognition for his intervention.

After these events, King Ahasuerus promoted a very evil person named Haman and advanced him above all others in his kingdom. He was basically the king's "second-in-command." All the king's servants were commanded to bow and pay homage to Haman as a form of worship. But Mordecai refused. Incidentally, Haman was an Agagite and may have been a descendant of the Amalekites, who were the enemies of the Jews. (See Exodus 17:8-16 and Deuteronomy 25:17-19.) He was from the Persian province of Agag.

Now Haman became so outraged that he devised a scheme to kill all the Jews in revenge against Mordecai. A *Pur*, or lot, was cast for the day of the annihilation of the Jewish people. The lot fell on the 13th of Adar on the Jewish calendar (February-March): "In the first month, which is the month of Nisan, in the twelfth year of King Ahasuerus, they cast Pur (that is, the lot), before Haman to determine the day and the month, until it fell on the twelfth month, which is the month of Adar" (Esther 3:7).

Haman offered King Ahasuerus ten thousand talents of silver to whomever would destroy the Jews. The king accepted Haman's scheme and issued a decree in his own name that he sealed with his signet ring. Letters were sent into all the provinces commanding the annihilation of all the Jews and the plundering of their possessions.

Esther 3:10, 13 reads, "So the king took his signet ring from his hand and gave it to Haman, the son of Hammedatha the Agagite, the enemy of the Jews....And the letters were sent by couriers into all the king's provinces, to destroy, to kill, and to annihilate all the Jews, both young and old, little children and women, in one day, on the thirteenth day of the twelfth month, which is the month of Adar, and to plunder their possessions."

When Mordecai heard the news, he tore his clothes and put on sackcloth and ashes, cried loudly, and went before the king's gate.

Wherever the decree was sent, the Jews mourned greatly, wept, and fasted. Esther heard that Mordecai was mourning and inquired as to the reason. She was given a copy of the king's decree to destroy the Jews as well as instructions from Mordecai to go before the king and intercede for her people.

Esther must have been struck with fear. She sent word to Mordecai that whoever enters the king's inner court without being called is subject to death. The king had not called for Esther in 30 days. Mordecai responded that Esther would not escape death any more than any other Jew and that perhaps the unseen hand of the Almighty had placed her in the kingdom for such a time as this.

> *"All the king's servants and the people of the king's provinces know that any man or woman who goes into the inner court to the king, who has not been called, he has but one law: put all to death, except the one to whom the king holds out the golden scepter, that he may live. Yet I myself have not been called to go in to see the king these thirty days."*
>
> *So they told Mordecai Esther's words. And Mordecai told them to answer Esther: "Do not think in your heart that you will escape in the king's palace any more than all the other Jews. For if you remain completely silent at this time, relief and deliverance will arise for the Jews from another place, but you and your father's house will perish. Yet who knows whether you have come to the kingdom for such a time as this?"* (Esther 4:11-14)

Esther understood the warning and sent word to Mordecai to gather all the Jews in Shushan to fast with her for three days and three nights. After that time, Esther would go against the law and present herself before the king. Esther 4:15-17 says, "Then Esther told them to reply to Mordecai: 'Go, gather all the Jews who are present in Shushan, and fast for me; neither eat nor drink for there days, night or day. My maids and I will fast likewise. And so I will go to the king, which is against the law; and if I perish, I perish.' So Mordecai went his way and did according to all that Esther commanded him."

On the third day, Esther prepared herself and went to the inner court of the king's palace. When the king saw his beautiful queen, she found favor in his sight. He extended his golden scepter to her, granting her permission to approach him. Esther touched the top of the scepter to show her gratitude. She then invited the king and Haman to a banquet she had prepared.

Haman became prideful and arrogant because he alone was invited to this special banquet with Esther and the king. Yet Mordecai was spoiling his party. Haman's wife and friends suggested he make a gallows from which to hang Mordecai the morning after the banquet. The gallows was to be 75 feet high so everyone could see it.

The Hebrew word for gallows is "tree." The tree Haman selected was in his own yard (see Esther 7:9). Haman planned to hang Mordecai from a 75-foot-tall tree in his own yard so everyone in the capital could see it.

The night before the banquet the king could not sleep. The king commanded that his book of chronicles be read to him. As it happened, the servant read the story of Mordecai uncovering the plot on the king's life. When the king learned that he had not rewarded Mordecai, he decided to honor him.

About this time, Haman had entered the outer court of the king's palace to suggest that the king hang Mordecai. The king asked Haman what he could do to honor a man in whom he delighted. Naturally, Haman thought the king was speaking about himself. Haman suggested that the man be clothed with one of the king's robes, given the king's horse with a royal crest, and paraded through the city.

Haman's face must have turned purple when the king instructed him to do just that for Mordecai (see Esther 6:10). His inflated pride burst. His heart sickened. His brow and the palms of his hands began to sweat. He was dumbfounded yet managed to stumble from the palace to fulfill the king's wishes.

Somehow, Haman was able to control his rage while leading Mordecai through the city on the king's horse proclaiming, "Thus shall it be done to the man whom the king delights to honor!" (Esther 6:11).

Later in the day, Haman's wife and friends said to him, "If Mordecai, before whom you have begun to fall, is of Jewish descent, you will not prevail against him but will surely fall before him" (Esther 6:13).

That night the king and Haman went to the banquet Esther had prepared for them. The king asked Esther what she wanted of him and said he would grant her request even if she wanted half of his kingdom. Esther revealed the plot against her people, including herself, and asked the king to spare them from the decree of death. The king did not know the plotter was Haman. When Esther revealed his identity, the king was so upset that he went into his garden to gather his wits.

Haman's anxiety caused him to violate palace etiquette and come too close to the couch where Esther was reclining to eat. When the king returned, he though Haman was trying to assault Esther. The king commanded that Haman be hung on the tree that he had prepared for Mordecai. (See Esther 7.)

The king gave Esther the house of Haman. When she told the king that she was Jewish and Mordecai was her relative, the king gave Mordecai his signet ring. Esther then appointed Mordecai over the house of Haman.

The king gave Mordecai the exalted position of Haman: "So Mordecai went out from the presence of the king in royal apparel of blue and white, with a great crown of gold and a garment of fine linen and purple; and the city of Shushan rejoiced and was glad" (Esther 8:15).

This was a great victory, but the decree could not be changed. However, the king instructed Mordecai and Esther to write a new decree permitting the Jews to defend themselves. A copy of the decree was sent to all the provinces so that the Jews would be ready on the day of the attack. Haman's law was in effect for 70 days, corresponding to the 70 years of captivity in Babylon. (See Esther 8.)

When the Jews heard the good news, they celebrated with a great feast and holiday. And they had nearly eight months to prepare themselves for the attack. When the attack came on the 13th, the Jews were ready. They slaughtered their enemies, and the Jews in the provinces celebrated on the next day. In Shushan, Esther received permission from the king for the Jews to also fight on the 14th. They killed the ten sons of Haman and hanged them on the gallows. Then all the Jews in Shushan celebrated on the 15th. (See Esther 9:1-17.)

As a result of this great victory, Mordecai declared Purim to be a holiday of feasting and joy, with presents being exchanged and gifts given to the poor. The people accepted Mordecai's words, and to this day, they celebrate Purim:

> *"And Mordecai wrote these things and sent letters to all the Jews, near and far, who were in all the provinces of King Ahasuerus, to establish among them that they should celebrate yearly the fourteenth and fifteenth days of the month of Adar, as the days on which the Jews had rest from their enemies, as the month which was turned from sorrow to joy for them, and from mourning to a holiday; that they should make them days of feasting and joy, of sending presents to one another and gifts to the poor. So the Jews accepted*

the custom which they had begun, as Mordecai had written to them" (Esther 9:20-23).

Purim gets it name from the *Pur* (lot) that was cast. It is generally celebrated on the 14th, but walled cities such as Jerusalem celebrate on the 15th. We notice from the text in Esther that the Jews established Purim as a day of celebration not just for themselves, but for all who would join them. This means that Christians are invited to celebrate this joyous occasion with the Jewish people. Without this victory, the Jews would have perished, and the Messiah would not have been born:

> *"So they called these days Purim, after the name Pur... the Jews established and imposed it upon themselves and their descendants and all who would join them, that without fail they should celebrate these two days every year, according to the written instructions and according to the prescribed time, that these days should be remembered and kept throughout every generation, every family, every province, and every city, that these days of Purim should not fail to be observed among the Jews, and that the memory of them should not perish among their descendants"* (Esther 9:26-28).

PURIM AND THE NEW TESTAMENT

While Purim is not specifically mentioned in the New Testament, it is most likely the feast John mentions when Jesus healed the man at the pool of Bethesda. The text reads, "After this there was a feast of the Jews, and Jesus went up to Jerusalem" (John 5:1). The next verses (2-15) tell about Jesus healing the man who had been sick for 38 years.

The reason we would understand this to be Purim is because it is the feast that is taking place before Passover, which is mentioned in the next chapter of John (see John 6:4). Both are called a feast of the

Jews or Judeans. Purim is celebrated on the Gentile calendar in February-March, while Passover follows in March-April. Even though Purim was not one of the biblical Feasts of the Lord, Jesus was in Jerusalem celebrating the feast.

If Jesus considered these festivals important enough for Him to celebrate, and since non-Jews are invited to join with them, it seems that Christians should be able to accept the invitation and find ways to participate while honoring Jesus.

Christians can certainly learn much from the story of Esther. First of all, we see that the wicked Haman prefigures satan and the "man of sin" known as the antichrist. Haman sought to kill God's ancient people. Likewise, Jesus speaks of satan as a thief who comes to steal, and to kill, and to destroy (see John 10:10).

The writer of the Book of Hebrews tells us that satan has the power of death (see Heb. 2:14). Surely Haman's plot to kill the Jews was inspired by satan, just as he will inspire and energize the false Messiah at the end of the age.

Esther speaks of "Haman the wicked." He had great power and was given authority over all the rulers in Persia. They were required to bow to him as an act of worship. Likewise, satan will give his power to the human beast who will force everyone to take his mark as a sign of worship (see Dan. 7:8; Rev. 13).

Haman's heart was filled with pride. He boasted of his glory and riches. So will the "man of sin" exalt himself above all that is called God (see 2 Thess. 2:4). Haman was the enemy of the Jews. The beast of Revelation will also seek to destroy the Jews (see Dan. 12; Matt. 24; Rev. 12).

Haman used his political power and cunning to betray Mordecai and as a pretense to destroy the Jews. In like manner, the false Messiah will use his political cunning and power to betray the Jews in a vain attempt to destroy them.

But like Haman, the false Messiah is also doomed. One day Haman was the "exalted one." The next day he was hanging from his own tree. The wicked one of Daniel and Revelation will also be exalted, but only for a brief time. He too will be destroyed by the coming of the true Messiah (see 2 Thess. 2:8; Rev. 19-20). The one more wicked than Haman will not prevail against Jesus but will surely fall before Him.

Like Mordecai, Jesus will be exalted and honored. He will wear the king's clothes, the king's crown will be on his head, and He will ride the king's white horse, the oriental symbol of victory. All those who hated God and His people will proclaim in every city square that Jesus is God's Messiah and Son in whom God delights. Every knee will bow and every tongue confess that Jesus is Lord to the glory of God the Father (see Phil. 2:9-11).

The Bible says that all of us are under a death sentence due to sin (see Rom. 6:23). Like the Jews of Persia, satan and sin seek to destroy us. Because of God's moral nature, His decree of judgment on sin cannot be revoked.

But God has not left us defenseless. He has written a new decree. It has been carried to all the provinces of the world by God's ambassadors of the New Covenant. It says, "For God so loved the world that He gave His only begotten Son, that whoever believes in Him should not perish but have everlasting life. For God did not send His Son into the world to condemn the world, but that the world through Him might be saved" (John 3:16-17).

As Esther interceded for her people, Jesus has interceded for us. He could have kept his identity secret, but He revealed Himself as the Jewish Messiah and Savior of the world. He not only fulfilled the role of Esther, but He also took the curse of Haman as He was hanged on a tree that should have been for us. That tree of the cross has been lifted high for the entire world to see.

Jesus interceded for us on the cross by taking the curse of sin for us. But while Esther presented herself on the third day to an immoral, unstable king, Jesus was resurrected from the grave at the end of three days and three nights and presented Himself to a holy God as atonement for sin. The writer of Hebrews tells us, "Therefore He is able to save to the uttermost those who come to God through Him, since He always lives to make intercession for them" (Heb. 7:25).

PERSONAL APPLICATION

How can Christians apply the Feast of Purim to our lives? Is Purim just some old "Jewish holiday," or is there a truth or lesson for those of us who are non-Jewish believers and disciples of Jesus? We can apply the Feast of Purim to our lives in three ways.

1. Fast and Pray

Christians should be like Mordecai and Esther. We should mourn, fast, and pray when the wicked are exalted. We should pray and work to fight the spiritual powers that would seek to exalt the wicked and destroy the righteous.

The often quoted Scripture says, "If My people who are called by My name will humble themselves, and pray and seek My face, and turn from their wicked ways, then I will hear from heaven, and will forgive their sin and heal their land" (2 Chron. 7:14).

Isaiah wrote the great chapter on fasting. God spoke these words through the prophet, "Is this not the fast that I have chosen: to loose the bonds of wickedness, to undo the heavy burdens, to let the oppressed go free, and that you break every yoke?" (Isa. 58:6).

2. Intercede for the Jewish People

As Esther and Mordecai and Jesus interceded for their own brethren, so Christians should intercede for the Jewish people. The Psalmist wrote, "Pray for the peace of Jerusalem: 'May they prosper who love you'" (Ps. 122:6).

Isaiah declared for the Lord, "I have set watchman on your walls, O Jerusalem; they shall never hold their peace day or night. You who make mention of the Lord, do not keep silent, and give Him no rest till He establishes and till He makes Jerusalem a praise in the earth" (Isa. 62:6-7).

3. Get Involved

Our intercession for Israel should be more than just prayer. The Bible says that God will use the Gentiles to help the Jews return to their land at the end of the age.

Isaiah wrote, "Behold, I will lift My hand in an oath to the nations, and set up My standard for the peoples; they shall bring your sons in their arms, and your daughters shall be carried on their shoulders....Surely the coastlands shall wait for Me; and the ships of Tarshish will come first, to bring your sons from afar, their silver and their gold with them, to the name of the Lord your God, and to the Holy One of Israel, because He has glorified you" (Isa. 49:22; 60:9).

Like Esther, perhaps we have come into the Kingdom of God for such a time as this. God has commissioned us to help our elder brothers, the Jewish people, return to their land. If we do not help, God will bring them deliverance from another source. But we must not be deceived to think that we, who have become part of the commonwealth of Israel, will be able to sit on the sidelines and watch without being noticed by the modern Hamans of our world.

PERSONAL STUDY REVIEW

1. Explain the historical background of Purim.

2. Explain how Jesus relates to the story of Purim.

3. How can you apply what you have learned in this lesson to your life?

ENDNOTE

1.   John Alexander Hammerton, "Susa: The Eternal City of the East," in *Wonders of the Past* (New York, NY: Wise &, 1937), 697.

CHAPTER 10

HANUKKAH

We learned in the previous chapter that the Feast of Purim was not one of the original Feasts of the Lord. It was a minor holiday commemorating the deliverance of Jews from Persia in the fifth century B.C. by Esther and her cousin Mordecai.

Likewise, Hanukkah has historically been a minor festival commemorating the great victory of the Jews over Antiochus Epiphanes in the second century B.C. The word *Hanukkah* means "dedication" and refers to the time when the Jews rededicated their temple after defeating Antiochus. However, the background to this story began several hundred years earlier with Alexander the Great.

HISTORICAL BACKGROUND

There has never been a ruler like him. He conquered more of the known world, in less time, with more lasting impact than any ruler before or after him. Alexander's father, Philip, became king of Greece by force. Christians know of him because of the letter written by the apostle Paul to a group of Christians in a city named after Philip. It was called Philippi.

When Philip died, Alexander succeeded him and began a brief, but spectacular, career of conquest that lasted not much more than a decade (336–323 B.C.). Alexander did the impossible. He conquered the mighty Persian Empire. In 333 B.C., Alexander met and defeated the Persian king Darius III in a decisive battle at Issus. He then entered Syria and conquered all of the Middle East, including Israel and Egypt, where he built the city of Alexandria.

After subduing Egypt, Alexander returned to the East and occupied the great Persian capitals of Babylon and Susa. He pushed as far as the Indus River in India, where his troops became homesick and forced him to turn back west. In 323 B.C., while laying plans for future battles, Alexander died suddenly of a fever in Babylon at the young age of thirty-three.

Alexander's most important victory was not of a military nature. His greatest conquest was spreading Greek culture, Greek language, and a Greek world-view. This process is called "Hellenism," based on the ancestral name of the Hellenic race of people who came to be known as the Greeks.

Alexander was tutored by Aristotle, who planted the dream in young Alexander's mind of a one-world civilization united by Greek culture, Greek language, and the Greek way of life. This ideal motivated Alexander to conquer the world for Greece. He sought to share his glorious culture and language with the rest of humanity, if they wanted it or not.

Alexander did this by establishing Greek as the common language throughout the known world and by building Greek city-states where he incorporated Greek culture, Greek literature and philosophy, Greek religion with its many gods, Greek customs, and the Greek way of life. Sooner or later these were bound to clash with God-fearing Jews in Israel.

Alexander died without making the necessary arrangements for a successor. Following his death, Alexander's generals fought for control of the empire. It was eventually divided into four parts, each governed by one of his generals. One general was given the area of Macedon and Greece, another Thrace and Asia Minor, the third Syria and Babylon, and the fourth was given Egypt.[1]

The general who ruled over Egypt was named Ptolemy. He established a powerful dynasty that prospered under him and his successors. The last and most famous of the Ptolemic rulers was Cleopatra, who ruled independently through the support of Julius Caesar and Mark Antony until her death in 30 B.C. At this time the Ptolemic dynasty came to an end.

The general who ruled over Syria was named Seleucus. He also established a powerful empire with Antioch as the most important city in his kingdom. Antioch was destined to become the first major non-Jewish center of Christianity (see Acts 11:19-26) and the head-quarters from which Paul left on his missionary journeys.

As was common in ancient times, the Seleucid kings were worshipped as gods. They also spread the Hellenistic dream of Alexander. The Seleucid Empire gradually diminished and was annexed by Rome in 64 B.C.

The Seleucids and Ptolemies constantly fought each other in an attempt to expand their respective empires. For more than a hundred years, the little land of Israel was caught in a power struggle between them. Some of their battles are mentioned in the Book of Daniel (see Dan. 11) where the Seleucids are called the "king of the north" and the Ptolemies the "king of the south." At times, the Plotomies were victorious and ruled over Israel while at other times the Seleucids were the victors.

When Antiochus IV Epiphanes (175–164 B.C.) came to the Seleucid throne, his empire was stronger than the Ptolomies'. He was the most oppressive and cruelest of the Selucid kings, and he was determined to spread Hellenism throughout his empire.

Antiochus made a systematic attempt to replace Jewish faith and culture with Greek culture. He was determined to destroy the Jewish people through assimilation. Antiochus forbade the Jewish people to practice their religion. They could not practice circumcision, observe the Sabbath, celebrate the feasts, keep their dietary laws, study the Torah, or in any way worship the God of Abraham, Isaac, and Jacob.

Antiochus stopped the temple ritual and ordered the burning of the Torah. He erected a statue to Zeus, in the temple and built a new altar dedicated to Zeus on which he offered a sacrificial pig. This was prophesied by Daniel and is recorded in Daniel 11:31. Antiochus thought himself to be the manifestation of Zeus, which is why he called himself *Epiphanes* which means "God manifest." Antiochus then poured the pig's blood over the Torah.

He erected shrines and altars throughout the land, and the people were forced to offer sacrifices as tokens of their acceptance of the new religion. Those who disobeyed were either tortured or killed or both. Their bodies were mutilated, and while still alive and breathing, they were crucified. The wives and sons whom they had circumcised were strangled. They were then crucified with the dead bodies of their children made to hang around their parent's necks.[2]

We learn of these events in the Books of First and Second Maccabees, which were written during this period of time. While these books are not an inspired part of the Bible, they do help us understand these important events.

First Maccabees reads, "Then the king wrote to his whole kingdom that all should be one people, and that all should give up their particular customs. All the Gentiles accepted the command of the king. Many even from Israel gladly adopted his religion; they sacrificed to idols and profaned the Sabbath. And the king sent letters by messengers to Jerusalem and the towns of Judah; he directed them to follow customs strange to the land, to forbid burnt offerings and sacrifices and drink offerings in the sanctuary, to profane Sabbaths and festivals, to defile the sanctuary and the priests, to build altars and sacred precincts and shrines for idols, to sacrifice swine and other unclean animals, and to leave their sons uncircumcised.

> "They were to make themselves abominable by every thing unclean and profane, so that they would forget the law and change all the ordinances. He added, 'and whoever does not obey the command of the king shall die'" (1 Maccabees 1:41-50).

We learn further, "Now on the fifteenth day of Chislev, in the one hundred forty-fifth year [167 B.C.], they erected a desolating sacrilege on the altar of burnt offering. They also built altars in the surrounding towns of Judah, and offered incense at the doors of the houses and in the streets. The books of the law that they found they tore to pieces and burned with fire. Anyone found possessing the book of the covenant, or anyone who adhered to the law, was condemned to death by decree of the king. On the twenty-fifth day of the month they offered sacrifice on the altar that was on top of the altar of burnt offering. According to the decree, they put to death the women who had their children circumcised, and their families and those who circumcised them; and they hung the infants from their mothers' necks" (1 Maccabees 1:54-61).

Regrettably, many of the leaders in Israel, especially from the upper class, embraced Hellenism. However, soon a revolt began led by an aged priest named Mattathias, from the family of Hasmon.

First Maccabees tells the following story, "The king's officers who were enforcing the apostasy came to the town of Modein to make them offer sacrifice. Many from Israel came to them; and Mattathias and his sons were assembled. Then the king's officers spoke to Mattathias as follows: 'You are a leader, honored and great in this town, and supported by sons and brothers. Now be the first to do what the king commands, as all the Gentiles and the people of Judah and those that are left in Jerusalem have done. Then you and your sons will be numbered among the Friends of the king, and you and your sons will be honored with silver and gold and many gifts.'

"But Mattathias answered and said in a loud voice: 'Even if all the nations that live under the rule of the king obey him, and have chosen to obey his commandments, every one of them abandoning the religion of their ancestors, I and my sons and my brothers will continue to live by the covenant of our ancestors. Far be it from us to desert the law and the ordinances. We will not obey the king's words by turning aside from our religion to the right hand or to the left.'

"When he had finished speaking these words, a Jew came forward in the sight of all to offer sacrifice on the altar in Modein, according to the king's command. When Mattathias saw it, he burned with zeal and his heart was stirred. He gave vent to righteous anger; he ran and killed him on the altar. At the same time he killed the king's officer who was forcing them to sacrifice, and tore down the altar. Then Mattathias cried out in the town with a loud voice, saying, 'Let everyone who is zealous for the law and supports the covenant come out with me!' Then he and his sons fled to the hills and left all that they had in the town" (1 Maccabees 2:15-25, 27-28).

The family that led the revolt was given the name "Maccabees." It is unclear how this name originated. Some say it is an acrostic created by combining the first letter of the Hebrew words that means, "Who among the mighty is like You?" A second view is that the word "maccabee" is derived from the Hebrew word for "hammer," which is a picture of great strength. Judah, the leader, was therefore called the Maccabee because of his great strength.[3]

Mattathias died shortly after the beginning of the revolt, but his five sons, of whom Judah Maccabee was the leader, carried on a guerrilla struggle. They were joined by many, including some of the "Hasidim" who were loyal to the traditional religion and way of life.

The army of Antiochus was much larger and more powerful than the righteous remnant of Israel. Looking at the situation in the natural, there was no way Judah and his fighters could have defeated Antiochus. However, God was with His covenant people. Judah displayed extraordinary skills as a leader, military tactician, and diplomat. With help from the Almighty, he succeeded in defeating Antiochus and won the struggle for religious freedom.

In 164 B.C., exactly three years after the altar to Zeus had been set up, the temple was cleansed, and the daily burnt offering and other religious ceremonies resumed. That rededication of the temple is still commemorated each December as Hanukkah, the Feast of Lights.[4]

Once again we turn to First Maccabees: "Early in the morning on the twenty-fifth day of the ninth month, which is the month of Chislev, in the one hundred forty-eighth year, [164 B.C.], they rose and offered sacrifice, as the law directs, on the new altar of burnt offering that they had built. At the very season and on the very day that the Gentiles had profaned it, it was dedicated with songs and harps and lutes and cymbals. All the people fell on their faces and worshipped and blessed Heaven, who had prospered them.

> "So they celebrated the dedication of the altar for eight days.... Then Judas and his brothers and all the assembly of Israel determined that every year at that season the days of dedication of the altar should be observed with joy and gladness for eight days, beginning with the twenty-fifth day of the month of Chislev" (1 Maccabees 4:52-56,59).

Traditional Jewish writings tell us that the Greek-Syrians desecrated all the oil purified for temple use. When the temple was rededicated, only one small undefiled container was found with the seal still on it. It contained only enough oil to burn the menorah for one day. But after the menorah was kindled, it miraculously burned for eight days. A more likely reason it was celebrated for eight days is because Hanukkah was originally called the "Succot of the month of Chislev" (as mentioned in Second Maccabees 1:9 and 10:6-8). *Succot* is celebrated for eight days. However, since the Maccabees were in hiding on *Succot* and could not properly observe it, they celebrated the holiday later when they were victorious.[5]

HANUKKAH AND THE NEW TESTAMENT

While Hanukkah was not a required biblical feast day, it was celebrated as a minor holiday, as we have just read in the Book of Maccabees. It was called the Feast of Dedication, and later, the Feast of Lights. Jesus must have participated in the celebration, as we learn in the Gospel of John, "Now it was the Feast of Dedication in Jerusalem, and it was winter. And Jesus walked in the temple, in Solomon's porch" (John 10:22-23).

How interesting that Jesus was at the temple during the very feast that celebrated the Jews' victory over the enemies of God as well as the rededicating and lighting of the temple. It was also on this occasion that some of the Jewish religious leaders in Jerusalem asked Jesus to tell them if He was the Messiah. Since this was during the Hanukkah celebration, perhaps they had in mind their ancestors' victory over Antiochus and were expecting the Messiah to lead them into battle against the Romans and restore their religious and political freedoms. Jesus answered their question by saying, "...I told you, and you do not believe. The works that I do in My Father's name, they bear witness of Me" (John 10:25).

In His first coming, Jesus did not come to defeat the Romans. He came to defeat the enemies of our soul. He came to defeat sin, satan, and death. He came to establish a spiritual kingdom in the hearts of mankind. This was a victory greater than what the Maccabees could achieve.

Jesus demonstrated this spiritual victory by His miracles and His resurrection. These were the works that bore witness to Him as the long-awaited Messiah. Jesus will defeat the enemies of God in the political realm at His second coming when He will establish the Kingdom of God and the kingdom of David on the earth.

Because Jesus is able to deliver us from an enemy more powerful than Antiochus, He is certainly greater than Judah the Maccabean. The New Testament gives the following witness of Jesus, "...God anointed Jesus of Nazareth with the Holy Spirit and with power, who went about doing good and healing all who were oppressed by the devil, for God was with Him" (Acts 10:38)

Peter adds in his letter that "[Jesus] who has gone into heaven and is at the right hand of God, angels and authorities and powers having been made subject to Him" (1 Pet. 3:22).

Paul writes, "Therefore, God also has highly exalted Him and given Him the name which is above every name, that at the name of Jesus every knee should bow, of those in heaven, and those on earth, and of those under the earth, and that every tongue should confess that Jesus Christ [Yeshua the Messiah] is Lord, to the glory of God the Father" (Phil. 2:9-11).

Jesus is not only our Deliverer; He is also the true Light of God. John said that Jesus was the true Light that gives light to every man coming into the world: "There was a man sent from God, whose name was John. This man came for a witness, to bear witness of the Light, that all through him might believe. He was not that Light, but was sent to bear witness of the Light. That was the true Light which gives light to every man coming into the world" (John 1:6-9).

Jesus Himself claimed to be that Light. He said, "As long as I am in the world, I am the Light of the world" (John 9:5).

Furthermore, Jesus made the following astonishing claim that totally baffled those listening. He said, "Destroy this temple, and in three days I will raise it up" (John 2:19).

Jesus was not talking about the literal temple, which had taken forty-six years to build. He was talking about His body. Through His resurrection and ascension, He would build a spiritual temple made up of people whose lives would be dedicated to God. We are that spiritual temple, and we have received His life and power to overcome the Hellenistic world in which we live.

It is possible that Jesus, God's true Light, was conceived during Hanukkah, the Feast of Lights. According to Luke 1:5, Zacharias was a priest of the division of Abijah. Luke 1:8-11 says that Gabriel appeared to Zacharias when he was serving as a priest in the temple.

Based on Rabbinic writings, the division of Abijah served as priests during the second half of the fourth month on the Jewish religious calendar. It was then late June when Elizabeth conceived John the Baptist.[6]

According to Luke 1:24-26, Mary conceived Jesus in the sixth month of Elizabeth's pregnancy. This means that Jesus was conceived during the latter part of the Jewish month of *Kislev*, or late December on the Gentile calendar. Jesus was born nine months later, most likely during the Feast of Tabernacles.

Forty days after Jesus was born, He was dedicated to His heavenly Father at the temple. It was there that Simeon said that Jesus was a light to bring revelation to the Gentiles, and the glory of Israel (see Luke 2:32). God's true Light had come into the world to reveal His Father to us.

PERSONAL APPLICATION

Can Christians apply the Feast of Hanukkah to our lives? Are there any truths or lessons we can learn? Most definitely! Jesus said to His followers, "You are the light of the world. A city that is set on a hill cannot be hidden. Nor do they light a lamp and put it under a basket, but on a lampstand, and it gives light to all who are in the house. Let your light so shine before men, that they may see your good works and glorify your Father in heaven (Matthew 5:14-16).

We can be God's lights and apply the Feast of Hanukkah to our lives in three ways: 1) separate ourselves from the godless world system in which we live (in the world but not of the world), 2) dedicate ourselves (the spiritual temple of God) to the Lord, and 3) trust God to help us overcome the enemies of our soul, which are more powerful than we are in the natural.

1. Separate Ourselves from the World

John writes these words to the followers of Jesus, "Do not love the world or the things in the world. If anyone loves the world, the love of the Father is not in him. For all that is in the world—the lust of the flesh, the lust of the eyes, and the pride of life—is not of the Father but is of the world. And the world is passing away, and the lust of it; but he who does the will of God abides forever" (1 John 2:15-17).

2. Dedicating Ourselves to God

Paul writes, "I beseech you therefore, brethren, by the mercies of God, that you present your bodies a living sacrifice, holy, acceptable to God, which is your reasonable service. And do not be conformed to this world, but be transformed by the renewing of your mind, that you may prove what is that good and acceptable and perfect will of God" (Rom. 12:1-2).

> "Or do you not know that your body is the temple of the Holy Spirit who is in you, whom you have from God, and you are not your own? For you were bought at a price; therefore glorify God in your body and in your spirit, which are God's" (1 Corinthians 6:19-20).

3. Trusting God to Help Us Overcome Our Spiritual Enemies

John wrote, "You are of God, little children, and have overcome them, because He who is in you is greater than he who is in the world" (1 John 4:4).

PERSONAL STUDY REVIEW

1. Explain the historical background of Hanukkah.

2. Explain how Jesus fulfilled Hanukkah.

3. How can you apply what you have learned in this lesson to your life?

ENDNOTES

1. "Alexander the Great," Wikipedia, Division of the Empire, accessed June 30, 2015, https://en.wikipedia.org/wiki/Alexander_the_Great.

2. "Antiochus IV, Epiphanes," JewishEncyclopedia.com, accessed June 30, 2015, http://www.jewishencyclopedia.com/articles/1589-antiochus-iv-epiphanes.

3. "Maccabees," Wikipedia, The revolt, accessed June 30, 2015, https://en.wikipedia.org/wiki/Maccabees.

4. "Hanukkah," Wikipedia, Traditional view, accessed June 30, 2015, https://en.wikipedia.org/wiki/Hanukkah.

5. Ibid.

6. David R. Reagan, "When Was Jesus Born?" Lamb and Lion Ministries, accessed June 30, 2015, http://www.lamblion.com/articles/articles_first3.php.

CHAPTER 11

HOW CHRISTIANS CAN CELEBRATE JESUS IN THE FEASTS

People all over the world are searching for their roots. Likewise, Christians are searching for their spiritual roots. More and more believers around the world are discovering the vital connection between Christianity and Judaism that existed severed centuries ago. Once that severing took place, biblical Judaism and biblical Christianity, which God intended to be one, went their separate ways.

Now we are living in a new prophetic season when the Lord is calling Christians and Jews back to their biblical roots. The biblical root of Christianity is Jewish. This root grew from an everlasting covenant God made with Abraham. Christians become part of that root through our faith in Jesus as the Jewish Messiah, Savior, and Lord.

Many believers who are discovering their roots want to celebrate the biblical Feasts of the Lord as they point to Jesus. You may think of these as "Jesus Fests." Way back in the 1970s when the

Lord touched so many people's lives, we just couldn't get enough of Jesus. We were so excited about our love relationship with Him that we wanted to celebrate Him all the time. So we had concert/festivals where people from many different Christian traditions came together to sing and pray and share our personal testimonies. It was wonderfully refreshing.

From a Christian view, the Feasts of the Lord are Jesus Fests. I have been celebrating them for many years. This has greatly enriched my life and the lives of others that I have had the blessing to teach. Over the years, people have asked me how to celebrate the feasts. For this reason, I have included this chapter with some basic suggestions and guidelines. These are just some initial ideas to get you started. If you want further assistance, you may contact our office, and we would be honored to serve you.

CELEBRATING THE FEAST OF PASSOVER (PESACH)

We have learned that what Christians have traditionally called "The Last Supper" was really Jesus celebrating Passover with His disciples. It was also the "Covenant Meal" symbolizing Jesus giving His life for and to His disciples. The Church ordinance of "Communion" has its roots in this meal.[1]

The church in Corinth consisted primarily of non-Jewish believers. Yet, Paul wrote to them, "Therefore purge out the old leaven, that you may be a new lump, since you truly are unleavened. For indeed Christ [Messiah], our Passover, was sacrificed for us. Therefore let us keep the feast, not with the old leaven, nor with the leaven of malice and wickedness, but with the unleavened bread of sincerity and truth" (1 Cor. 5:7-8).

Paul considered Passover a Feast of the Lord for all of God's people, not just the Jews. So how can Christians celebrate Jesus in the Passover? The obvious way is to have a Passover meal as a picture pointing to Jesus our Passover Lamb. The Passover meal is the visual aid helping us to "see" the Passover story in Exodus and in the Gospels.

We read in the Exodus story that the Lord told His covenant people to keep the Feast of Passover as an everlasting memorial (see Exod. 12:14). For centuries parents told the story to their children orally. But later when the Jews were scattered among the nations, they saw the need to write down the story. Eventually they added some rituals to the memorial and developed a uniform order of service called a *Seder*. The word *Seder* means "order."

The Passover *Seder* is written so everyone present can follow along. I have written a Christian-friendly *Seder* called "Passover *Seder*: A Christian Remembrance of Passover." It serves as the teaching tool showing how Jesus fulfilled the Feasts of Passover, Unleavened Bread, and Firstfruits. This is a unique *Seder* beautifully illustrated with color symbols and an explanation of the common elements on the memorial plate. You may order it from my ministry Website. Using material like this will serve both to guide and to enhance your own celebration of Passover—whether you are celebrating as a family or as a congregation.[2]

CELEBRATING THE FEAST OF PENTECOST (SHAVUOT)

We have learned that God told the people to bring a sheaf of the firstfruits and wave it before Him for 50 days. This was from the Feast of Firstfruits to the Feast of Pentecost. Since the Hebrew word for sheaf is *omer*, the period of time between these two feasts is called the time of the Counting of the *Omer*. As I mentioned, the counting always started at day one and continued until day fifty as follows: Today is the first day of the *omer*, today is the second day of the *omer*, today is the third day of the *omer*, etc.

Since we are all easily distracted, counting the *omer* helped the people keep their focus on the Lord and His special feast days. It was a reminder of what the Lord had done for them at Passover, and it looked forward to what He did for them at Pentecost. He redeemed them at Passover and gave them the Torah at Pentecost. Because the period in between these two feasts took place during the time of the story of Ruth and Naomi and Boaz, Jewish people traditionally read the Book of Ruth when celebrating the Feast of Pentecost.

Christians can also embrace the days of the Counting of the *Omer* because we too are easily distracted by the things and cares of the world. We too need spiritual pictures and visuals to keep us connected to what the Lord has done for us. Rather than watching television, we can do something a lot more exciting. We can count the *omer*. But instead of literally counting the *omer*, we can read selected Scriptures for each of the 50 days between the Feast of Firstfruits and the Feast of Pentecost. This will keep us focused and connected on what Jesus has done for us in fulfillment of these feasts.

I have included below a possible Scripture-reading plan for you to follow for each of the 50 days. It conveniently includes reading Psalm 119 and the Book of Acts. You can look on any Jewish calendar on the internet or otherwise and see when Firstfruits and Pentecost are on the calendar for any given year.

COUNTING THE OMER THROUGH SCRIPTURE READING			
DAY	SCRIPTURE READING	DAY	SCRIPTURE READING
1	Psalm 119:1-8	26	Acts 4
2	Psalm 119:9-16	27	Acts 5
3	Psalm 119:17-24	28	Acts 6
4	Psalm 119:25-32	29	Acts 7
5	Psalm 119:33-40	30	Acts 8

COUNTING THE OMER THROUGH SCRIPTURE READING			
6	Psalm 119:41-48	31	Acts 9
7	Psalm 119:49-56	32	Acts 10
8	Psalm 119:57-64	33	Acts 11
9	Psalm 119:65-72	34	Acts 12
10	Psalm 119:73-80	35	Acts 13
11	Psalm 119:81-88	36	Acts 14
12	Psalm 119:89-96	37	Acts 15
13	Psalm 119:97-104	38	Acts 16
14	Psalm 119:105-112	39	Acts 17
15	Psalm 119:113-120	40	Acts 18
16	Psalm 119:121-128	41	Acts 19
17	Psalm 119:129-136	42	Acts 20
18	Psalm 119:137-144	43	Acts 21
19	Psalm 119:145-152	44	Acts 22
20	Psalm 119:153-160	45	Acts 23
21	Psalm 119:161-168	46	Acts 24
22	Psalm 119:169-176	47	Acts 25
23	Acts 1	48	Acts 26
24	Acts 2	49	Acts 27
25	Acts 3	50	Acts 28

The Feast of Pentecost is a perfect time to plan a Summer Jesus Festival. It would be appropriate for the family or the minister to read or give a sermon based on Acts 2, including an explanation of the biblical background of the feast. This could be followed by a time of thanksgiving and praise, calling on the Holy Spirit to fill all those present as He did on the Day of Pentecost. Three thousand responded to Peter's message and were baptized that day. This would be a great time to baptize new converts.

Since Pentecost was a harvest festival, it would be appropriate to bring bread and canned food items to give to the church pantry for the needy as a wave offering to the Lord. The people could bring a total of 50 loaves and actually wave these to the Lord as they present them. The Book of Ruth could be read or dramatized. An outdoor concert with Tabernacle of David worship along with a church picnic could be planned as part of the service. These are just a few suggestions.

CELEBRATING THE FEAST OF TRUMPETS (ROSH HASHANAH)

We have learned that the Feast of Trumpets was on the first day of the seventh month on the religious calendar. Recall that this is the Hebrew month of *Tishri,* which corresponds to the months of September-October on the Gentile calendar. *Tishri* is also the first month on the Jewish civil calendar and is the Jewish New Year. In Hebrew, the word *Rosh* means head or beginning and *HaShanah* means "the year." So the Hebrew name for this beginning of the year is *Rosh HaShanah.*

Because the main activity on this day is the blowing of trumpets, it is called in Hebrew *Yom Teruah,* the Day of Sounding the Trumpet. Whereas Gentiles celebrate the New Year with revelry, in the Jewish tradition, the Feast of Trumpets is a call to a spiritual awakening, spiritual warfare, and repentance that culminates ten days later on the Day of Atonement, *Yom Kippur.*

In actual practice, the Jewish people began preparing for the Day of Atonement the month prior to *Tishri.* This is the month of *Elul,* which is August-September on the Gentile calendar. Jewish tradition teaches that Moses went up to meet with God on Mount Sinai at the beginning of *Elul* and returned 40 days later on the Day of

Atonement. In view of this, the *shofar* is blown in the synagogue each morning of the 30 days of *Elul* plus the ten days from *Rosh HaShanah* to *Yom Kippur*. This gives a total of 40 days of preparation as the sound of the *shofar* calls the people to repentance. The Hebrew word for repentance or return is *teshuvah*.[3] It is also believed that the sound of the *shofar* frightens the devil. So it is an instrument of warfare as well as repentance and revelation.

The *shofar* sound is one of the most haunting sounds you can hear from an instrument. I suppose this is because the *shofar* is "God's instrument of choice" in the Bible. *The Encyclopedia of Judaism* says that the *shofar* "calls upon sinners to repent, awakens thoughts of God's sovereignty, justice and redeeming power, and expresses the Jew's hope that God will before long 'sound the great shofar' to herald deliverance and the ingathering of the exiles in the land of Israel."[4]

Rabbi Wayne Dosick comments that the sound of the shofar on *Rosh Hashanah* "serves as a warning to people to wake up out of their lethargy, to scrutinize their deeds, to improve their conduct; it serves as a prelude to the announcement of God's judgment, and it serves as a reminder that one day, the Kingdom of God—the time of the Messiah—will be announced to the whole world."[5]

Moses Maimonides was one of the greatest of Jewish sages. He wrote of the symbolic significance of the *shofar* with these words, "Awake, O you sleepers, awake from your sleep! Search your deeds and turn in repentance. O you who forget the truth in the vanities of time and go astray all the year after vanity and folly that neither profit nor save—remember your Creator! Look at your souls, and better your ways and actions. Let every one of you abandon his evil ways and his wicked thoughts and return to God so that He may have mercy on you."[6]

In the New Testament, the apostle Paul wrote in a similar vein, "...Awake, you who sleep, arise from the dead, and Christ [Messiah] will give you light" (Eph. 5:14).

The *shofar* is so important that the Bible says that the Lord Himself will blow it when He comes to redeem His people: "Then the Lord will be seen over them, and His arrow will go forth like lightning. The Lord God will blow the trumpet [*shofar*], and go with whirlwinds from the south" (Zech. 9:14). I think you can see from these statements just how important the *shofar* is to the Lord.[7]

Because the Lord provided a ram as a substitute for Isaac in the story of Genesis, it is customary for Jewish people to read Genesis 22 on *Rosh HaShanah*. In Hebrew, the story of the binding of Isaac is called *akeidah*.[8] Jewish tradition teaches that God preserved the two horns of the ram that took Isaac's place. He sounded the smaller horn at Mount Sinai when He gave them the Torah and will sound the larger horn for redemption at the coming of Messiah.[9] Wow! Any Christian should be able to see the connection between the sacrifice of Isaac and the sacrifice of Jesus, who will sound the great *shofar* at His coming.

In connection with repentance and seeking God for forgiveness, the Jewish people have a very powerful visual aid tradition called *Tashlich*. This Hebrew word means "casting or throwing." The ceremony involves gathering at a body of flowing water and symbolically "casting" their sins into the water to be carried away by the current. The worshiper does this by throwing bread crumbs or small pebbles into the water.[10] This dramatic act gets its inspiration from Micah 7:19, which reads, "He will again have compassion on us, and will subdue our iniquities. You will cast all our sins into the depths of the sea."

Jewish tradition teaches that God seals the names of the righteous on *Rosh HaShanah* and reveals their destiny ten days later on *Yom Kippur*. No wonder they greet one another with the phrase *Shanah tovah*, meaning, "May it be a good year," or the more spiritual greeting *L'shanah tovah tikatevu*, meaning, "May you be inscribed (in the Book of Life) for a good year."[11] For Jewish people, the ten-day period between *Rosh HaShanah* and *Yom Kippur* is the time to do many good deeds (*mitzvot*) in hopes that God will see their efforts and include them in the Book of Life.[12]

In keeping with this same theme, Jewish people celebrate *Rosh HaShanah* by eating apples dipped in honey. This is another visual aid that symbolizes their hope for a sweet new year. A typical prayer at this time is, "May it be Your will, O Lord our God, that we be renewed for a good and sweet new year."[13]

It should be obvious after reading this how Christians can celebrate this wonderful feast day. If you have the budget, you can buy a *shofar* and blow it at home. They come in all sizes and prices, and the family will enjoy it. You don't have to know how to blow the *shofar*; just blow it as a reminder of all it means.

You can also read the appropriate Scriptures, such as the use of trumpets in Numbers 10 and the story of Joshua and the battle at Jericho. You can have your own *Tashlich* service while reading Micah 7:19 and Psalm 103:12. You can read the New Testament Scriptures about Jesus overcoming His temptations from the devil in Matthew 4 and other Scriptures, such as Paul's instructions to put on the armor of God in Ephesians 6. You can make sweet apples, honey cakes, etc., and greet each other with the appropriate greetings. You are only limited by your own creativity and imagination. You can read Revelation 4 and 5 and thank God that your names are written in the Lamb's Book of Life. Hallelujah!

CELEBRATING THE DAY OF ATONEMENT (YOM KIPPUR)

Remember from Leviticus 16 that the Day of Atonement was the one day the High Priest went into the Holy of Holies and offered the blood on the Ark of the Covenant as atonement for the sins of the people. Because of the sobering nature of this event, the Day of Atonement is considered the most solemn day on the biblical calendar. In fact, it is the only required fast day in the Bible.

The Day of Atonement is a day of "afflicting our souls," which is Bible talk for humbling ourselves before God. James was referring to this when he wrote, "Draw near to God and He will draw near to you. Cleanse your hands, you sinners; and purify your hearts, you double-minded. Lament and mourn and weep! Let your laughter be turned to mourning and your joy to gloom. Humble yourselves in the sight of the Lord, and He will lift you up" (James 4:8-10).

Wow! That sure clarifies the purpose of *Yom Kippur.* As the Bible puts it, this is a day of "sackcloth and ashes." It is a day of coming to God with a broken spirit and a contrite heart. It is a day of seeking God's grace and mercy for the forgiveness of our sins and the ability to endure our trials and sufferings.

Because of the serious nature of this time on the calendar, the ten days from *Rosh HaShanah* to *Yom Kippur* are know as the Days of Awe, *Yamim Noraim* in Hebrew. Of all the feasts, these religious holy days are called the High Holidays or High Holy Days. More Jews will attend the synagogue during these religious observances than any of the other feast days throughout the year. This is the one time of the year Jews get serious with God even though they may not have given Him much thought otherwise.[14]

The Jewish people have a powerful prayer book called the *Siddur.* I encourage every Christian to buy a copy. Of course the prayers do not reference Jesus, but they are profound prayers from the Hebrew Bible. The best known prayer is called *Kol Nidre,* which means "all vows." It is a haunting prayer to God in which worshipers ask God to show them mercy by canceling all vows they were not able to fulfill during the year.

The *Siddur* also contains a long prayer that includes human "short-comings" for which the worshiper seeks forgiveness. Judaism understands that the Almighty will not forgive the people's sins unless they are right with each other. So this is a time of forgiving each other for offenses incurred.

There is an ancient Jewish custom on *Yom Kippur* called *Kaparos*, meaning atonement. In this ritual, the worshiper take a white rooster for males and a white hen for females and twirls it over his or her head three times while reciting the following prayer: "This is my exchange, this is my substitute, this is my atonement. This rooster (for males) or hen (for females) will go to its death while I will enter and go to a good, long life, and to peace."[15]

I have quoted this prayer directly from the *Siddur.* For Christians, the connection to Jesus is obvious. His blood has made atonement for our sins. His death on our behalf was the once-and-for-all sacrifice. We don't need the blood of a chicken or any other animal to cover our sins. But we do sin, and we need to seek God for forgiveness based on the blood of Jesus.

John makes the following statement that Christians can use as their *Yom Kippur* prayer, "If we say that we have fellowship with Him, and walk in darkness, we lie and do not practice the truth. But if we walk in the light as He is in the light, we have fellowship with one another, and the blood of Jesus Christ [Yeshua the Messiah] His Son cleanses us from all sin. If we say that we have no sin, we deceive ourselves, and the truth is not in us. If we confess our sins, He is faithful and just to forgive us our sins and to cleanse us from all unrighteousness" (1 John 1:6-9).

In addition to seeking forgiveness from God, this is a good time to forgive those who have harmed you and seek forgiveness from those you may have harmed. Of course, we should do this whenever we are aware of the need. But just in case we have neglected to tend to this important command from the Lord, *Yom Kippur* is a good time to make things right.

Jesus spoke clearly about the necessity of forgiveness. He said, "For if you forgive men their trespasses, your heavenly Father will also forgive you. But if you do not forgive men their trespasses, neither will your Father forgive your trespasses" (Matt. 6:14-15). God has forgiven us the great debt of sin. Since He has forgiven us so a great debt, we certainly should forgive others the relatively small debt they owe us.

Yom Kippur is a good time for Christians to read Leviticus 16 through 17 and the account of the crucifixion of Jesus in the Gospels. It is a good time to confess our sins to the Lord and to one another. It is a good time to repent, accept the blood of Jesus as our basis for forgiveness, and begin a sweet new year with the Lord and our loved ones.

CELEBRATING THE FEAST OF TABERNACLES (SUCCOT)

The Feast of Tabernacles has such universal significance in God's redemptive program that He requires all nations to go to Jerusalem to celebrate this feast during the Millennium (see Zech. 14:16). Many thousands of believers are doing so today as a sign of the prophetic season in which we are living.[16]

If you are not able to go to Jerusalem, you can have your own *Succot* party at home. You can build a booth and display it during services or at home. Building a *succah* (booth) is a wonderful family project. Dad or the men in the congregation could build the frame (three sides and roof). Remember to construct the roof open enough to see through to the sky. A lattice or trellis roof works fine. The fourth side is the door. Mom or the women in the congregation can add colorful bedspreads or sheets to the sides. The children can participate by decorating the booth with streamers, fruit, lights, etc. You can cover the roof with leafy branches, pine or palm branches, etc. Be sure and set the booth in an accessible place for the entire week of Tabernacles. Spend some time in the *succah*. Have a meal and fellowship along with prayer and Scripture reading, games, etc.

The Feast of Tabernacles is a time of great joy and pageantry. This is a great opportunity to read the background to the Feast of Tabernacles from Leviticus and John 7:37-39. Along with an appropriate teaching and Bible reading, family members or the congregation can get involved by making banners (see Ps. 20:5). There can be a parade of banners accompanied by joyous Tabernacle of David praise and worship. The banners can be displayed for the entire week.

Since the Feast of Tabernacles represents the millennial kingdom, it would be appropriate to have a teaching on what life will be like during this time on earth. A city-wide parade could be planned for the afternoon with many churches participating. This could culminate in a joint praise and worship service at a central gathering place, such as a park or stadium.

CELEBRATING THE FEAST OF PURIM

Purim is a day of rejoicing and celebrating. Basically, it is a party. Since Purim is based on the story recorded in the Book of Esther, the Jewish people read the Book of Esther.

Our Jewish friends have a lot of fun when reading Esther. Since Haman represents their arch enemy, whenever his name is read, they boo and hiss, stomp their feet, and sound noisemakers called *groggers* to drown out the mention of his name. They cheer at the mention of Mordecai. In our own Christian celebration of Purim, I have added "oohing and ahing" at the mention of Esther. We bring noisemakers to drown out the mention of Haman and then to cheer for Mordecai. You can see that Purim can be a lot of fun.

Jewish people send gifts to their friends and contribute to the poor, as recorded in the Book of Esther. A special pastry called "Haman's ears" is prepared. It has three corners and is usually filled with poppy seeds or other fillings. You can purchase these at any Jewish bakery during Purim. In some circles, Purim is celebrated in a carnival atmosphere with masquerades, costumes, and a lot of celebrating. A good time is had by all.

Children love this celebration because they can play games, eat lots of goodies, and dress up as the biblical characters in the Book of Esther. Food baskets can be prepared, and gifts can be exchanged as a way of celebrating.

In addition to the above, you can have a dramatic presentation of the Book of Esther. As Christians, we can also read the story of Jesus in Jerusalem healing the man at the Pool of Bethesda as recorded in John 5. The possibilities are limited only by your imagination.

CELEBRATING HANUKKAH

Although Hanukkah has been celebrated for centuries, it has only been in recent times that it has gained importance. This is probably because of the need for the Jewish people to have an alternative to Christmas, since Hanukkah and Christmas are both celebrated in December.

The central focus in celebrating the eight days of Hanukkah is lighting the eight-branched menorah called a *hanukkiah*. *Hanukkiahs* are available at any Jewish gift shop. The *hanukkiah* has a ninth candle called a *shamash*. This word means "servant." The servant candle is used to light the other eight. The candles are placed in the *hanukkiah* each evening from right to left, with a new candle added each evening during the eight-day celebration. The candles are lit from left to right. So the *shamash* is lit first, and then the others are lit.

From a Christian perspective, Jesus is the Servant Light who lights our lives with the fire of God when we receive His Spirit into our lives. Jesus said, "As long as I am in the world, I am the light of the world" (John 9:5). When His life is burning brightly in us, we are human *hanukkiahs* bringing glory and honor to our Lord.

We recall that Jesus said to His followers, "You are the light of the world. A city that is set on a hill cannot be hidden. Nor do they light a lamp and put it under a basket, but on a lampstand, and it gives light to all who are in the house. Let your light so shine before men, that they may see your good works and glorify your Father in heaven" (Matt. 5:14-16).

It would certainly be acceptable for Christians to purchase a *hanukkiah* and light it during Hanukkah as a picture of the person. Once again, this is a visual way of keeping us connected to our Lord.

Three special blessings are said on the first evening before lighting the *shamash*. After the blessings are said, you light the candles and begin your celebration. The first two are said each evening thereafter. A Christian desiring to celebrate Hanukkah may offer the following blessings:

> "Blessed are You, O Lord our God, King of the universe, who has sanctified us through Messiah Jesus, our true Light."

> "Blessed are You, O Lord our God, King of the universe, who has wrought miracles to save the Jewish people in order to give us the Messiah."

> "Blessed are You, O Lord our God, King of the universe, who has kept us alive, sustained us, and brought us to this season."

Hanukkah can be a very exciting time for Christians. You can read the story of Jesus celebrating Hanukkah as recorded in John 10. You can celebrate with special songs, food, and games. There are many parties, and lots of gifts are exchanged. This is the time to tell the story of the Maccabees and the miracle that tradition tells us God performed. It's also another opportunity to put on a play followed by a party and time of thanksgiving to the Lord. Family members can play Hanukkah games.

A special game played on Hanukkah is called *dreidel*. A *dreidel* is a four-sided top that is spun. Each side of the *dreidel* holds a Hebrew letter. The four letters form an acrostic that means "A great miracle happened there." In Israel, the last word is changed to here. The winner of the *dreidel* game gets the most Hanukkah *gelt* (chocolate money). As we spin the *dreidel*, we are reminded of the great miracles that happened in Jerusalem 2,000 years ago when Jesus walked the earth.

On Hanukkah, the foods are cooked in oil as a reminder of the miracle of the oil when the Temple was rededicated. Many households eat potato pancakes called *latkes* and jelly-filled doughnuts fried in oil to commemorate the occasion. Even this can be a visual reminder that we are to be filled with the "oil of the Holy Spirit."

CELEBRATING THE SABBATH

The purpose of this book is to teach how the seven biblical Feasts of the Lord are pictures pointing to Jesus. Many Christians have also discovered this about the Sabbath.

One of my books, *Shabbat Shalom,* explains in a "Christian-friendly" manner what the Hebrew Bible says about the Sabbath, the Sabbath between the Testaments, Jesus and Paul and the Sabbath, the Sabbath and the New Testament Church, and the Sabbath for Christians in today's world. In the last part of this practical book, I explain in clear, easy-to-follow steps how Christians can honor the Lord and celebrate the Sabbath in their home.

Thousands of Christians have had their lives changed and their families strengthened by reading this book and practicing what they learned. You can order this book from my Website. It is a great resource. You will learn how to make your family meals a time of worship and how to pray blessings over your family. By celebrating Jesus in the Sabbath, your home can be a temple of God, your table an altar to the Lord, and your life a song to God.[17]

PERSONAL STUDY REVIEW

The fact that you have read this book means that the Lord is stirring you to learn about the biblical Hebraic roots of our Christian faith. As He puts the desire in your heart, you will want to celebrate Jesus in the Feasts of the Lord as well as Purim and Hanukkah. While this will certainly mean some adjustments in your calendar and family life, the blessings and rewards are great. Begin now to plan and organize for the next feast on the calendar. And please contact us if we can serve you as you begin this exciting journey.

ENDNOTES

1. Over 30 years ago I wrote a book on the covenant. *The Miracle of the Scarlet Thread* became a worldwide best-selling classic on this subject. I am forever grateful to God for choosing me to write the book. You may order it from my online bookstore.

2. Along with the printed publication, I have made a recording of a live presentation on an audio CD. There are several ways you can use this material as a guide to having your own Passover service.

   First, you can order the CD and printed Seder and listen and read for yourself. Second, you can order the CD and a copy of the Seder for each family member. If you choose this option, you can all listen together to the CD while each follows along in his or her own printed Seder. For example, if you have five family members, you would need the one CD and five printed Seders.

   Finally, I have the complete Seder in a professional PowerPoint presentation, which I am available to give at your congregation. If you are interested, you can order the CD and printed Seder from my online bookstore. You may contact my office to discuss the possibility of my coming to your congregation to present the Seder in person.

3. "Repentance," JewishEncyclopedia.com, accessed June 30, 2015, http://www.jewishencyclopedia.com/view.jsp?artid=216&letter=R.

4. Geoffrey Wigoder, ed., *The Encyclopedia of Judaism* (New York: Macmillan Publishing Company, 1989), 653.

5. Wayne Dosick, *Living Judaism* (New York: HarperCollins, 1995), 133.

6. Yechiel Eckstein, *What Christians Should Know about Jews and Judaism* (Waco, TX: Word, Inc., 1984), 119.

7. If you want to know more about the shofar, you can order my book entitled *The Shofar: Ancient Sounds of the Messiah.*

8. Staff, "Ado-nai," Orthodox Union, June 19, 2006, https://www.ou.org/judaism-101/glossary/a-donai/

9. "The Binding of Isaac," Kehilat Sar Shalom, accessed June 30, 2015, http://www.rabbiyeshua.com/articles/2001/akeidah.html.

10. Ariela Pelaia, "Tashlich: What Is Tashlich?" About.com, accessed June 30, 2015, http://judaism.about.com/od/roshhashana/a/shana_tashlich.htm.

11. John J. Parsons, "Rosh Hashanah: Awakening to Judgment," Hebrew for Christians, accessed June 30, 2015, http://www.hebrew4christians.com/Holidays/Fall_Holidays/Rosh_Hashannah/rosh_hashannah.html.

12. Dovid Bendory, "The Book of Life," Pidyon, April 28, 2006, http://rabbi.bendory.com/audio/teshuva/teshuva12.php.

13. Parsons, "Rosh Hashanah."

14. John Dart and Regina Hong, "New Beginnings for High Holy Days," Los Angeles Times, September 19, 1998, http://articles.latimes.com/1998/sep/19/local/me-24322.

15. "Kaparos," The Jewish Outreach Institute, accessed June 30, 2015, http://www.joi.org/celebrate/yomkippur/kaparos.shtml.

16. If you want to go to Jerusalem to celebrate the Feast of Tabernacles, please contact us to learn about our tours or see our Website.

17. For information on how Christians can celebrate Jesus in the Sabbath, please order my book, Shabbat Shalom, available from the online bookstore at www.rbooker.com.

CELEBRATING JESUS IN THE PASSOVER

A Christian-friendly practical guide
for conducting a Passover Seder

We are living at a time in redemptive history when the Lord is working to bring true spiritual unity to the church in order to manifest His Kingdom on the earth. God is bringing this unity in a number of different ways. One of the primary ways is by emphasizing our common Hebraic roots and heritage.

While there are many things that divide the church, no matter what our differences we all share a common heritage in the death, burial, and resurrection of Jesus. The one event in the life of Jesus that most clearly symbolizes this redemptive work, and with which all Christians can identify, is Passover.

DO THIS IN REMEMBRANCE OF ME

It was Jesus Himself who said, "Do this in remembrance of Me." Luke writes:

When the hour had come, He sat down, and the twelve apostles with Him. Then He said to them, "With fervent desire I have desired to eat this Passover with you before I suffer; for I say to you, I will no longer eat of it until it is fulfilled in the kingdom of God." Then He took the cup, and gave thanks, and said, "Take this and divide it among yourselves; for I say to you, I will not drink of the fruit of the vine until the kingdom comes." And He took bread, gave thanks and broke it, and gave it to them saying, "This is My body which is given for you; do this in remembrance of Me." Likewise He also took the cup after supper, saying, "This cup is the new covenant in My blood, which is shed for you" (Luke 22:14-20).

Christians rightly understand the bread and cup to represent the communion meal with our Lord. Yes, it is the covenant meal. It is the ultimate and most intimate expression of "I'm in you and you're in Me; the two of us have become one." By taking the bread and the cup we are expressing our spiritual union with God. For believers, it is our most sacred act of worship.

When we internalize communion in Spirit and in truth, the Lord is able to manifest His presence in us in the most remarkable ways. In an act of faith and worship, we exchange our liabilities (human failings) for His assets (the Holy Spirit in us ministering the life of Jesus to us).

I have learned that the best time to receive a miracle from God is when we take communion. This may be a new thought for many, but when you take communion in a worthy manner, ask for and expect God to do something significant in your life. First, repent of any known sins, and then make a verbal and spiritual exchange of your need for His supply. For years I have given communion with this understanding, and people have testified to all sorts of healings.

PASSOVER: IT'S NOT JUST A "JEWISH THING"

Christians can and should take communion whenever they want, but notice that the context of the very first Lord's Supper or communion or the covenant meal is Passover. Jesus offered the bread and the cup at Passover. He said it was His desire to eat the Passover with His disciples and that He would eat it again when He returned to establish the fullness of His Kingdom on the earth. This means that Passover is not just a "Jewish feast," but it is the Lord's Feast that not only looks back to His death, burial, and resurrection but also looks forward to His coming as King of kings and Lord of lords.

Jesus is not still on the cross; He is on the throne of authority in Heaven and coming again. Passover, communion, or the covenant meal is not just a funeral service where we mourn the death of Jesus for our sins. It is that but so much more. It is also a celebration of the fact that Jesus conquered sin, satan, and death and is returning to rule the nations in righteousness and peace. Believers will rule with Him.

Furthermore, Jesus not only gave His life for us (at Passover), He also gave His life to us (at Pentecost), and He is coming again to be with us at Tabernacles. Wow! Did you get that? You might want to read that sentence again and really meditate on it. Contemplating this should certainly fill us with great joy. We can enjoy His presence *now*—in our life here on earth—we don't have to wait until we "go to Heaven."

For now, Jesus has put His overcoming Spirit in us. As we understand that we are seated with Him in Heaven, His victory in Heaven is in us on the earth, our initial sorrow over what He suffered for us gives way to celebrating what He has done in us and to us and through us (see Rom. 6-8).

Christians are grafted into the Jewish people through a Jewish Messiah Lord and Savior (see Rom. 11:17–24). We are part of the Commonwealth of Israel (see Eph. 2:11–13). Jesus is returning as the

Lion of the Tribe of Judah and the greater Son of David (see Rev. 5:5). Christians will celebrate Passover with Him when He returns. Therefore it is not only appropriate for Christians to celebrate Passover; the New Testament Scriptures assume that we will. We look back to His death, burial, and resurrection, and we look forward to His return.

The apostle Paul wrote the following words to the believers in Corinth. They were primarily Gentiles who were not living holy lives but were keeping Passover. Paul did not rebuke them for keeping a "Jewish feast." He rebuked because they were keeping Passover without putting away their sins.

Here is what he said:

> *Therefore purge out the old leaven [put away your sins], that you may be a new lump [a holy people], since you truly are unleavened [a people forgiven and made new by God]. For indeed Christ [Messiah], our Passover, was sacrificed for us. Therefore let us keep the feast, not with old leaven, nor with the leaven of malice and wickedness, but with the unleavened bread of sincerity [pure motives of heart] and truth* (1 Corinthians 5:7-8).

For decades, I have taught Christians about our connection to Passover through Jesus our Passover Lamb. All Bible-believing ministers have done this. As the Lord began to awaken believers around the world to their Hebraic roots, many came to me expressing a desire to celebrate Passover but they didn't know how. As a result, I wrote a Passover guide for Christians which I am including here to assist those who want to celebrate Passover. It is a Christian-friendly, Jesus-centered presentation. I have written it in a non-technical way using the KISS method (Keep It Simple Saints).

There are prayers in Hebrew which may be a challenge to some. Not to fear! If you want assistance, I have available a Christian

Passover Seder package of four beautiful, fully-illustrated color booklets along with an audio CD of my presentation. You can order this package and have a Passover right in your own home with family and friends. You can either play the CD and follow along with it in your booklets, or you can learn it yourself. Whatever works best for you.

You can order the Christian Passover set from my website at www.rbooker.com. I am also available to personally lead your Passover service at your congregation or study group. I have the entire teaching in a beautiful PowerPoint presentation. If this is of interest to you, call our office in Texas at 936-441-2171. Now let's get started.

SOME PRELIMINARIES

Jewish homes use a Passover plate that has a place where you put special symbols. If you do not have one, you can purchase one from many different online sites.

The special symbols which I will explain later are:

1. Zeroah

2. Betzah

3.   Maror

4.   Karpas (parsley)

5.   Charoset

6.   Chazeret—optional. Some Passover plates have an extra place for a piece of romaine lettuce which is considered a bitter vegetable.

There are numerous recipes for making *charoset* which you can find on the Internet. A simple one is to use one cup of chopped walnuts, one chopped green apple, two teaspoons of cinnamon, two teaspoons of sugar, some spices, and red wine or grape juice to moisten the mixture. Mix and stir to a consistency and color of mortar for making bricks.

Other special symbols are:

1.   Matzah—to eat plus three pieces that you will place in a tri-fold napkin

2.   A tri-fold napkin—insert one piece of matzah in each of the three folds.

3.   Cups of salt water—place as many as needed on the table so people can reach them easily.

4.   Cups or small bowls for hand washing—place as many as needed on the table so people can reach them easily.

5.   Wine or grape juice bottle(s)

6.   Wine or grape juice cups or glasses for people to drink from. These would be placed at each person's plate.

7.   Saucers for each person with parsley and horseradish

8. Candles with matches or lighter

9. A cup for Elijah and empty place and chair for him to sit

WHAT TO EAT: THE MEAL

Because this a biblical meal, you would not want to serve pork or shellfish or, in this case, leavened bread.

Some suggestions are:

- Matzah ball soup if possible

- Matzah to eat as the bread

- Meat—lamb, chicken, turkey

- Vegetables, couscous, rice, etc.

- Bowl of charoset

- Dessert

- Appropriate beverage

THE ORDER OF SERVICE

We know that the Lord told the Hebrews to tell the Exodus story to their children so it could be passed down from one generation to the next (see Exod. 12:26–28). Just think, the Jewish people have been observing Passover for almost 3,500 years. And we get to join them. But how? This is what Jews in times past asked.

You see, as they were scattered among the nations, they needed to put in writing a standardized order for observing the Passover. So around A.D. 220, Jewish religious leaders added some rituals and developed a uniform order of service called a *Seder* ("order"). The Seder is a printed guide to tell the Passover story. Because the

Hebrew word for "story" is *haggadah*, the guide is called, "The Hagga´dah" or "Haggada´h."

Welcome to Our Passover Seder!

We begin by welcoming each person to the Christian celebration of the biblical feast of *Pesach* (Passover). This *haggadah* (story) will serve as our instruction manual as we take part in the same meal that Jesus or Yeshua observed with His disciples the night on which He was betrayed.

As we remember the mighty miracles God worked to redeem Israel from Egypt, may we rejoice in the same God who has redeemed us by the precious blood of His Son Yeshua/Jesus, who still works mighty miracles in our lives today! Hallelujah! As the Jewish people personally identify with the Exodus story, so we also personalize the spiritual aspects of redemption to our own lives through Yeshua/Jesus our Passover Lamb.

Learning the Symbols

On each table you will find a plate containing the common elements of a Passover Seder. As you will see, each of these elements is symbolic and helps us remember God's miracle of redemption from Egypt and our own lives through the death, burial, and resurrection of Yeshua/Jesus.

Zeroah (a lamb shank bone)

This reminds us of the lamb's death and blood which was applied to the doorpost of the Jews' homes at the first Passover. As believers, the shank bone is a clear visual of Yeshua/Jesus, our human Passover Lamb who gave His life and shed His blood for us. His blood applied to the "doorpost of our heart" delivers us from bondage to sin, satan, and the fear of death.

Betzah (roasted egg)

A later non-biblical symbol, the hard-boiled egg reminds us of both mourning and hope—mourning the destruction of the Temple, and hope for the spiritual restoration of the Jewish people. It pictures the agony and suffering Yeshua/Jesus endured for us, the mourning we share over His suffering on our behalf, and the hope of the resurrection. The cross is bare, the tomb is empty—Jesus is alive and He lives in us. Hallelujah!

Maror (bitter herbs)

Horseradish, and sometimes lettuce, is used to portray the bitterness of slavery in Egypt. It also pictures the bitterness of Yeshua/Jesus bearing our sins on the cross and the sorrow we should have when we fall short of God's expectations for us.

Salt Water

This reminds us of the tears the Hebrews shed in Egypt. As the perfect Hebrew of Hebrews, Yeshua/Jesus wept over the city of Jerusalem and was a man of sorrows. Likewise, believers should certainly weep tears of sorrow over the condition of the world and our own sins.

Karpas (Parsley)

This symbolizes the hyssop with which the blood was applied to the lintels and doorposts of the Hebrew's homes. Hyssop carries water in the stem. So when the blood was applied to the doorpost, water oozed out of the stem and sealed the blood in the doorpost. Likewise, when Yeshua/Jesus was crucified, blood and water poured out of His body to signify He really was dead. When we accept His death on our behalf, we are saved by His blood and sealed with the Living Waters of the Holy Spirit.

Charoset

This is a mixture of nuts, spices, and juice. Its red appearance reminds us of the red clay from which the Hebrews were forced to make bricks in Egypt. The bitter sweet taste in our mouth reminds us of the bitterness of what Jesus endured for us but also the sweetness of His resurrection. Once again, we have sorrow for the bitterness of sin in our lives but rejoice in the sweetness of forgiveness and reconciliation through the death, burial, and resurrection of Yeshua/Jesus.

Matzah (unleavened bread)

Matzah is the main element of any Passover Seder. It symbolizes the unleavened bread which the Jews ate with haste the night before their deliverance from Egypt. The *matzah* is pierced and bruised and has stripes. What a clear picture of our Lord who was pierced, bruised, and given lashes of stripes in His body.

Now that we've looked at the elements, we are ready to begin!

LIGHTING THE FESTIVAL LIGHTS

It is traditional for the mother of the home to light the festival lights. As we welcome this Holy Day by lighting candles, let us ask the Spirit of God to illumine us by His presence, bringing the fullness of meaning to our Passover experience. Let's observe now as the candles are lit and the blessing is given:

"Baruch Atah Adonai, Eloheinu Melech ha'olam, asher kidshanu be-mitzvotav, vetzivanu l'hadlik ner shel Pesach."

"Blessed are You, O Lord our
God, King of the universe,
Who has sanctified us by Your commandments
and inspired us to kindle the lights of Passover."

BLESSING OVER THE CHILDREN

At this time the Father of the family blesses his children. Let us now say the traditional blessing for sons:

"May the Lord make you like Abraham, Isaac, and Jacob."

And to the daughters, Father gives the following blessing:

"May the Lord make you like Sarah, Rebekah,
Rachael, and Leah."

The father then says the Aaronic priestly blessing (Num. 6:24–26) over his family, which we can recite together:

"The Lord bless you and keep you;
The Lord make His face shine upon you,
and be gracious to you;
The Lord lift up His countenance upon you,
and give you peace."

KIDDUSH: DRINKING THE CUP OF SANCTIFICATION

We will drink from the cup four different times. Based on Exodus 6:6-7, the cups are called the Cup of Sanctification, the Cup of Thanksgiving, the Cup of Redemption, and the Cup of Praise.

We now set apart (sanctify) this special meal with the Cup of Sanctification. As we pour the first cup, let us reflect on how our very lives are to be "Kiddush," sanctified for the glory and purposes of God. Let us now pour our cup, raise it in our right hand, and listen to the following blessing and then drink the cup:

"Baruch Ata Adonai, Eloheinu Melech ha-olam,
boray p'ree hagafen."
"Blessed are you, O Lord our God,

King of the universe,
who creates the fruit of the vine."

It is traditional to have several hand washings during a Seder. For the sake of time, we will have just one. In Psalm 24 David said:

"Who may ascend the hill of the Lord, or who may stand in His holy place? He who has clean hands and a pure heart."

Let's listen to the traditional blessing, and then we will wash our hands:

"Baruch Atah Adonai, Eloheinyu Melech ha-olam
asher kidshanu be-mitzvotav
vetzivanu at netilat yadadim."

"Blessed are You, O Lord our God, King of the universe, who has sanctified us by Your commandments and commanded us concerning the washing of hands."

KARPAS: EATING THE PARSLEY

The parsley reminds us of the hyssop used to apply the lamb's blood to the doorposts. The salt water reminds us of the tears the Hebrews shed in Egypt. Let's listen to the following blessing:

"Baruch Atah Adonai, Eloheinu Melech ha-olam,
boray p'ree ha'adomah."
"Blessed are You, O Lord our
God, King of the universe,
who creates the fruit of the earth."

We now dip the parsley in the salt water and partake.

YACHATZ: BREAKING THE MIDDLE MATZAH

Let's now remove the middle of the three cakes of *matzah*, known as the "Bread of Affliction." We break the *matzah*, take the larger piece and wrap it in a cloth to be hidden away until the end of the meal. Before the meal begins, someone should hide the hidden *matzah* somewhere in the room. Later, the children will be asked to search for it. If you have more than one family participating, you can designate one person to hide the *matzah* somewhere at the table such as under a plate.

We remember that Yeshua/Jesus was afflicted for us, wounded for our transgressions, and bruised for our iniquities. He is the true Bread of Life who was free from the leaven of sin. He was pierced for us and hidden away to be revealed at His resurrection and return.

MAGGID: TELLING THE PASSOVER STORY

In a traditional Jewish home the whole Exodus story is retold. The Lord commanded this in Exodus 12:26-27:

> *And when your children ask you, "What does this ceremony mean to you?" then tell them, "It is the Passover sacrifice to the Lord, who passed over the houses of the Israelites in Egypt and spared our homes when He struck down the Egyptians"* (NIV).

We now ask the famous question, "Why is this night different from all other nights?"

(Let us all recite the four responses):

1. On other nights we may eat either leavened or unleavened bread; this night we eat only unleavened.

2. On other nights we eat any kind of herbs; tonight we eat bitter herbs.

3. On other nights we do not dip even once; tonight we dip twice.

4. On other nights we eat sitting or reclining; tonight we recline.

DRINKING THE CUP OF THANKSGIVING

Another way in which we remember the Exodus is to recount the ten plagues with which God struck the Egyptians. God's Word teaches compassion toward one's enemies. With each plague mentioned we take a drop from the cup and put it on our plate to remember the suffering of the Egyptians.

Let's fill our cup again and recite the plagues together:

Blood - Frogs - Gnats (lice) - Flies - Pestilence (loss of cattle) - Boils - Hail - Locusts - Darkness - Firstborn slain

We now lift our second cup in our right hand and say together:

"Therefore we are bound to thank, praise, laud, glorify, extol, honor, bless, exalt, and reverence Him who performed for our fathers and for us all these miracles. He brought us from slavery to freedom; from sorrow to joy; from mourning to festivity, and from servitude to redemption. Hallelujah!"

Let's now drink the second cup and express our gratitude to the Lord by reciting the following traditional Passover declaration.

In Hebrew this is called *Dayenu,* which means, "it would have been enough." As followers of Yeshua/Jesus we have so much to be thankful for that any one thing He did for us would have been enough. But He has done so much more that we will spend eternity praising Him.

> *"If He had only redeemed us out of Egypt,*
>
> *and not brought judgment upon them,*
>
> *it would have been enough."*
>
> *"If He had only given to us the Sabbath,*
>
> *it would have been enough."*
>
> *"If He had only given to us the Torah,*
>
> *it would have been enough."*
>
> *"If He had only given to us the Messiah,*
>
> *it would have been enough."*

MOTZEE MATZAH: EATING THE MATZAH

Let's now take a piece of the matzah which we broke earlier, raise it together, and listen to the following blessing:

> *"Baruch Atah Adonai, Eloheinu Melech ha-olam,*
>
> *ha motzee lekhem meen ha-aretz."*
>
> *"Blessed are You, O Lord our God, King of the*
> *universe, who brings forth bread from the earth."*

(We all now eat a small piece of the matzah.)

MAROR: EATING THE BITTER HERBS

We eat bitter herbs to remind us of the bitterness of life of the Hebrews under the heavy yoke of slavery in Egypt. As we dip the *matzah* in the *maror*, we remember that we too have been redeemed from a heavy yoke of slavery to sin. Like the Israelites of old, we have been set free to serve God with our whole hearts.

Let's listen to the blessing, after which we will eat the *matzah* and *maror*.

"Baruch Atah Adonai Eloheinu Melech Ha'olam, asher
kidshanu bidevaro vetzivanu al akhilat maror."
"Blessed are You, O Lord our God, King of
the universe, who has set us apart by His Word
and commanded us to eat bitter herbs."

KORECH: EATING A SANDWICH

Let's now take two small pieces of matzah and dip them in both the *maror* and the *charoset*, making a sandwich!

The *charoset* is red and reminds us of the red clay the Israelites used to build bricks in Egypt. As we now eat the sandwich let us remember the bitterness of slavery but the sweetness of redemption.

SHULCHAN ORECH: EATING THE FESTIVE MEAL

The table is now spread for our Passover meal! In keeping with biblical tradition, we will say a blessing *after*, not before the meal (see Deut. 8:10). Enjoy *matzah*, *charoset*, and *maror* with the meal, but leave the *Afikomen* (hidden *matzah*) and wine/grape juice drink for later.

BARUCH: BLESSING GOD AFTER THE MEAL

Together: *"May the name of the Lord be blessed from now on and forever more. Blessed be our God, whose food we have eaten and through whose goodness we live."*

PSALM 126: READING A SONG OF ASCENTS

(Traditional reading following the festive meal.)

THE AFIKOMEN: FINDING THE HIDDEN MATZAH

In the Jewish home, this is the point where the children search for the *Afikomen*, the matzah which was broken then hidden away. Whichever child finds the hidden *matzah* receives a present forty days later from the father. This present is called, "The promise of the Father." This is the point of the Seder at which Yeshua/Jesus instituted the Lord's Supper or covenant meal with these words:

"This is My body which is given for you;

do this in remembrance of Me."

The *Afikomen* is another picture of Yeshua/Jesus, the unleavened Bread of Life, pierced for us. A blessing is now said, and the *Afikomen* is eaten.

"Baruch Atah Adonai, Eloheinu Melech ha-olam,

ha motzee lekhem meen ha-aretz."

(Let us now partake.)

DRINKING THE CUP OF REDEMPTION

"This cup is the new covenant in my blood,

which is shed for many for the remission of sins."

These were the Lord's words as He reached this point in the Seder. Let us have thankful, humble hearts as we celebrate redemption through His blood. Let's now fill the third cup and offer the following blessing:

"Baruch Atah Adonai, Eloheinu Melech ha-olam,

boray p'ree ha-gafen."

"Blessed are You O Lord our God,

King of the universe,

who creates the fruit of the vine."

(Let's now drink the third cup.)

SETTING ELIJAH'S PLACE

See, I will send the prophet Elijah to you before that great and dreadful day of the Lord comes (Malachi 4:5 NIV).

It is Jewish tradition that Elijah will return one year at this point in the Seder to fulfill Malachi 4:5. Just in case this is the year, an extra place setting is always put out, and the children go to the door to see if Elijah is outside waiting.

For believers in Messiah, we remember Yeshua's words in Matthew 11:14, *"And if you are willing to accept it, he* [John the Baptist] *is the Elijah who was to come."*

DRINKING THE CUP OF PRAISE

We now fill our cup a fourth time and recite one of the "Hillel" or "praise" Psalms, blessing God for His faithfulness. God is a faithful, covenant-keeping God who has bound Himself to us by the blood of the everlasting covenant in Yeshua/Jesus.

Leader: O give thanks to the Lord, for He is good!

Congregation: For His mercy endures forever!

Leader: Let Israel now say,

Congregation: His mercy endures forever!

Leader: Let the house of Aaron now say,

Congregation: His mercy endures forever!

Leader: Let those who fear the Lord now say,

Congregation: His mercy endures forever!

We now give the following blessing over the cup:

"Baruch Atah Adonai, Eloheinu Melech ha-olam,
borah p'ree ha-gafen"

(Let's now drink the Cup of Praise!)

Our Passover celebration is now complete. As we depart, let us take with us the depth and richness God has placed in this feast, as He has in all the biblical feasts.

May we live our lives with a renewed expectancy of His coming, a deeper passion for His presence, and a wholehearted love for our Passover Lamb, our Messiah Yeshua/Jesus who has redeemed us by His own blood and given us right standing before God.

Because Jerusalem is the ultimate home of all true believers, we conclude the Seder with the following traditional Hebrew phrase:

"L'shanah haba'ah bi Yerushalayim,"

which means:

Next Year in Jerusalem!

Institute for Hebraic-Christian Studies

4747 Research Forest Drive # 180-330

The Woodlands, TX 77381

Phone: 936-441-2171

www.rbooker.com

IHCS

email: shofarprb@aol.com

ABOUT THE AUTHOR

RICHARD BOOKER, MBA, PHD, is an ordained Christian minister, President of Sounds of the Trumpet, Inc., and the Founder/Director of the Institute for Hebraic-Christian Studies. Prior to entering the ministry, Richard had a successful business career. He is the author of thirty books and numerous seminars that are used by churches and Bible schools around the world.

Richard has traveled extensively for over thirty years teaching in churches and at conferences on various aspects of the Christian life as well as Israel and the Hebraic roots of Christianity. He and his wife, Peggy, have led yearly tour groups to Israel where, for eighteen years, Richard was a speaker at the International Christian Celebration of the Feast of Tabernacles in Jerusalem. This gathering is attended by 5,000 Christians from 100 nations.

Richard and Peggy cofounded the Institute for Hebraic-Christian Studies (IHCS) in 1997 as a ministry to educate Christians in the Hebraic culture and background of the Bible, to build relationships between Christians and Jews, and to give comfort and support to the people of Israel. Their tireless work on behalf of Christians and Jews has been recognized around the world as well as being represented at the Knesset Christian Allies Caucus.

Richard is considered a pioneer and spiritual father in teaching on Israel, Jewish-Christian relations, and the biblical Hebraic roots of Christianity. To learn more about his ministry, see his Website and online bookstore at *www.rbooker.com* or *www.soundsofthetrumpet.com*. If you would like Dr. Booker to speak at your church or congregation, you may contact him at *shofarprb@aol.com*.

Dr. Booker is available to present a Passover Seder at your church or congregation. Contact him at his ministry offices in Texas or send him an email at www.rbooker.com if you want to discuss this with him.